JOY SAMUELS, M.S., LPC/MH

WORKIN

CREATIVE

PLANNING

for the

SECOND

HALF OF LIFE

MW00861535

WORKING WITH GROUPS

CREATIVE PLANNING

for the

SECOND HALF OF LIFE

BURTON & DORIS KREITLOW

WHOLE PERSON ASSOCIATES
Duluth, Minnesota

Library of Congress Catalog Card Number: 96-60493
ISBN 1-57025-122-3

Printed in the United States of America

10 9 8 7 6 5 4 3 2 1

WHOLE PERSON ASSOCIATES
210 W Michigan
Duluth MN 55802-1908
800-247-6789

Dedication

This book is gratefully dedicated to 140 super elders whom we interviewed in the Midwest, Southeast, Hawaii, and England.

Chosen by your communities as models of a positive retirement, you became an inspiration for our own retirement. You taught us that race, wealth, and even health are not the most telling factors in the retirement phase of life's journey. Rather it is people, purpose, and continuing personal growth that builds the zest and joy in living. We hope this book passes your wisdom on to many others.

Acknowledgment

We acknowlege with deep gratitude the faith Donald Tubesing and Nancy Loving Tubesing had in our philosophy of retirement and the excellent editing of Susan Gustafson.

Contents

©1997 Whole Person Press 210 W Michigan Duluth MN 55802　(800) 247-6789

©1997 Whole Person Press 210 W Michigan Duluth MN 55802 (800) 247-6789

Introduction

We began studying retirement by design. Having always planned ahead, the knowledge that retirement was approaching five or ten years down the road triggered our first action. It was 1975, and we were spending a year at The Ohio State University (Burt as a Distinguished Visiting Professor, Doris as a staff writer for the Vocational Studies Center). A sabbatical offers time to think, so that's what we did.

Were we ready to retire? If knowledge of retirement was a prerequisite, we were not ready.

As a first step, we read what researchers and writers about gerontology were publishing. Their reports and articles were depressing, making retirement appear to be the end of the road. But, "Wait!" we said. These writers had looked only at the problems of retirement. Few of the retirees we knew fit the pattern described in these reports. Something was wrong.

In response, we began to study a group of positive retirees to learn what made them productive, happy people who were still growing well up into their eighties and nineties.

We were so enthusiastic about what we learned that we began to share our findings about positive retirees in local, regional, and national workshops and in preretirement meetings and conferences. By that time, we ourselves had retired, so we were able to speak both of our research and of our experiences.

This book, *Working with Groups: Creative Planning for the Second Half of Life*, was developed to distribute more widely the information we gathered and the learning

©1997 Whole Person Press 210 W Michigan Duluth MN 55802   (800) 247-6789

activities we have used to encourage thinking about retirement. The ideas and materials included in this book are designed to involve participants in thinking about the many creative alternatives available to each of us. There is no single answer best for everyone. There are choices to be made, and each should be made from the store of knowledge available. The information presented in this book, along with the suggested activities, will lead to better choices.

Moving a group into and through the readings and exercises can be a great experience for a leader. It can be a "fun" experience as well. No need to be a professional! The committee chair of a women's fellowship can be as effective as the church pastor. A social worker can do as well as a volunteer from the senior citizen's club. Persons "conned" into leadership roles in groups we have organized have been so effective they made us wish we could lead as well.

If you, the leader, find an exercise or report somewhere else that you think will work better for you, use it. Or if you do not like portions of the exercises we propose, create your own.

This book is an effort to prepare retirees to make choices that will lead to a great retirement. As you teach others, be sure also to plan for your own retirement.

©1997 Whole Person Press 210 W Michigan Duluth MN 55802 (800) 247-6789

Leader alert

Understanding the following characteristics of older adults will help leaders bridge the generation gap between leader and participants.

1. After age forty-five, hearing and visual acuity may decline. Consider this as you arrange seating, making sure that people will be able to hear you and each other. A sound system may be necessary if you are working with a large group. If you will be recording information on an easel pad, write boldly with a fresh, dark marker. Be sure that worksheets and handouts can be read easily.

2. Physical energy wanes, and comfort while sitting declines as we age. If a session is lengthy, a short stretch break will be needed.

3. Time pressures present barriers to clear thinking for older adults. Although small group activities must be conducted within certain time constraints, avoid announcing time limits for individual work.

4. Be prepared to allow for the decline in short-term memory that sometimes comes as we age. Long-term memory is generally good, and elders will be able to give good examples from life experiences.

For older leaders: The fact that you are a group leader suggests that your energy level is high and your adjustment to aging is exemplary. Although the four items listed above may not apply to you, try to keep them in mind and be understanding of those who are finding the aging process more difficult.

For younger leaders: To help you talk *with* your group rather than *at* them, put on an imaginery cloak of years and address the members as "we" rather than as "you" or "they." This little detail can help you work effectively with people much older than you. After all, no matter what our age, we are all in the process of aging, and we should all be planning for retirement.

For more information: Turn to the section: "How to use this book most effectively," which begins on page 174. It is filled with helpful tips on leading groups and on experiential learning.

©1997 Whole Person Press 210 W Michigan Duluth MN 55802   (800) 247-6789

Make the best retirement choices for the next century

1   Getting to know you

Use this two-part get-acquainted exercise at the start of a half-day or full-day workshop. **Part one** is a fun icebreaker. **Part two** will demonstrate to participants the varied ideas people have about retirement.

Objective

To help participants feel comfortable working together.

To learn about the likenesses and differences among group participants.

Group size

Fewer than 25 is preferable, but an experienced leader can work effectively with as many as 50 participants.

Time

Each part takes about 20 minutes. Do not allow either to run longer than 25 minutes.

Materials

Two blank 3" x 5" cards for each participant; paper and pencils; easel pad and markers.

Process

Part one

1. If this is the group's first meeting together, introduce yourself and explain that during this session, members will have an opportunity to meet each other and to learn about each other's hopes and plans for retirement years.

2. Distribute one 3" x 5" card to each participant and ask them, on the card, to describe in one or two sentences a significant life experience that occurred to them before

©1997 Whole Person Press 210 W Michigan Duluth MN 55802   (800) 247-6789

age thirty, one that others in the group are not likely to know about.

☞ *If anyone asks, "what kind of experience?" offer two or three examples, such as: "I shot a hole-in-one at age sixteen and none since," or "I was kicked out of high school for one week for drawing cartoons of the teachers."*

3. When everyone is finished, collect the cards, shuffle them, and as you redistribute the cards at random to participants, give instructions for the next step in the exercise.

➤ You will have 5 minutes to find the person whose experience is described on the card you were given.

➤ Determine who that person is, then, by asking questions, get as much information about that person as you can in the allotted time.

➤ When the 5 minutes are up, be prepared to introduce the person to the rest of the group.

4. After 5 minutes call "time," ask participants to be seated, and begin the introductions, reminding people to be brief. If it is clear from the size of the group that not everyone can be introduced, ask for volunteers. Be prepared to stop at the end of the 20-minute period allotted for this part of the exercise.

Part two

1. Distribute a second 3" x 5" card to each participant and give the following instructions:

➤ Those who are not yet retired should write on the card the one factor that you are most concerned about as you approach retirement.

➤ Those of you who are already retired should write on the card the one factor you were concerned about before retirement that was so easy to resolve you now can't figure out why you were concerned about it in the first place.

☞ *If asked for examples, give one or two, such as: "I didn't think I'd find enough to do to keep me busy," or "I didn't think the young person taking over my job would be able to do it right."*

2. Form groups of 4 to 6 participants, including retirees and preretirees in each group, if possible. Distribute paper and pencils to each group and provide the following instructions:

   ➤ Choose one group member to be the recorder for this exercise and another person to report the concerns of your group after the discussion period.

   ➤ Discuss your concerns about retirement with members of your group.

   ➤ List the concerns that are common to several members of the group on the paper you were given. You will have 6 minutes to complete this task.

3. As each group reports on its findings, summarize their responses on the easel pad.

4. Conclude the session with a 15-minute discussion on what people's responses show about the expectations and the realities of retirement.

   ☞ *If you would like to have another person do the written summary, arrange for this in advance. This will free you to concentrate on what people are saying.*

Variations

■ This exercise is particularly effective with a mixed group of retirees and preretirees. If the group comprises only preretirees, ask the small groups to discuss and compare their concerns about retirement. Retirees can be asked to compare their preretirement concerns with retirement realities.

■ **Part one** of this exercise can be used any time introductions are needed. The method described in **Part two** can help leaders and participants achieve a rough consensus on people's concerns about any topic and can help them plan future sessions targeted specifically to the group's interests and needs.

©1997 Whole Person Press 210 W Michigan Duluth MN 55802   (800) 247-6789

2 The changing world and you

The world does not stand still. By looking both backward and forward, recognizing the ever-accelerating rate of cultural and scientific change, people can prepare for a successful retirement. Because people today are living much longer, this generation will spend more years in the retirement world than previous generations even anticipated. We cannot predict the changes the next thirty years will bring, we can only make sure that we are ready.

Objectives

To understand the effects of recent changes in our culture.

To recognize the nature of the social and technological changes that we have resisted and those to which we adjusted quite easily.

To understand the continuing need for adaptations in today's world.

To understand the basis for variations in the way individuals within a cohort (age group) respond to societal, economic, and technological changes.

Group size

Unlimited. Works well with 20–40 participants.

Time

30–40 minutes. Longer if the variation is used.

Materials

Easel pad and markers.

Process

1. Introduce the changes that have taken place in retirees'

lifetimes by providing some of the following information along with your own insights.

- The world we were born into had disappeared before we retired.
- The Great Depression created a need for social change.
- World War II created a need for and the infrastructure for advancing technical change.
- Each cohort (age group) views the world from a different perspective. For example, most people who lived through the Depression and the World War II era have different views than Baby Boomers.
- Accelerating advances in the fields of electronics and communications continue to challenge any hopes we might have that change is slowing down.
- Today, if we retire at age sixty-five, we can expect to live another twenty or more years, and we can anticipate seeing more changes during that time than we witnessed in the previous twenty years.

2. Ask participants to respond with a show of hands to the following questions:
   - ✔ Did your mother drive a car regularly when you were a child?
   - ✔ Did you attend day-care or preschool as a child?
   - ✔ Did your family preserve its own food?

3. Ask participants to call out responses to the following questions:
   - ✔ What was the first car you recall being owned by your family?
   - ✔ What happened to children who were orphaned or who lost their mother?
   - ✔ When you were a child, what was your view of folks in their sixties and seventies?

✔ How much did you know about sex when you were ten years old?

4. To emphasize the rapid rate of social change, read the following lists quickly, asking for a show of hands in response to each, but not pausing to count or comment.

➤ Raise your hand if you were born before:

Man walked on the moon

Contact lenses

Credit cards

Automatic dishwashers

Doctors stopped making house calls

There were messages on T-shirts

Pantyhose

Air conditioners

➤ I'm going to read a list of things that today's fifteen-year-olds are familiar with. Raise your hand if you were aware of them when you were fifteen.

Most women have jobs

Designer jeans

Ballpoint pens

Windows 95

Laser beams

Computer programming

Social security

Cruise control

E-mail and the Internet

5. Summarize the responses with the following comments:

■ Yes, it was a different age. When the retired and those approaching retirement were young, every town had a 5 and 10 cent store; a nickel bought a coke, and coke was a cold drink; a postcard needed a one-cent stamp; a new car cost less than $600.00; gas cost less than today's gas tax; and rock music was Grandma's lullaby.

6. Ask participants the following question and record their responses on the easel pad.

✔ What do you believe to be the most significant social, scientific, and economic changes that have occurred during your lifetime?

☞ *Offer a few examples if needed: women's rights, communication, atomic energy, genetic engineering, one-world economy, ease of travel, computer chips, health care, social services, response to the environment, violence on TV.*

7. By asking for a show of hands, determine the five changes that are most significant to the group and place an * in front of them. Ask participants to decide whether the source of each of the five most significant changes was social, scientific, or economic.

8. Ask participants to brainstorm the social, scientific, and economic changes they anticipate during the next thirty years. On the easel pad, head three columns with the words *social, scientific*, and *economic* and record participants ideas under the appropriate headings. Tell them to be wild and free with their ideas.

9. Conclude the session by asking participants which changes they look forward to living with or using? Make a brief summary statement about the importance of being ready for and adapting flexibly to change.

Variation

■ An additional 30 minutes may be added to the session by discussing people's responses to the five most

©1997 Whole Person Press 210 W Michigan Duluth MN 55802 (800) 247-6789

significant changes identified in Step 7. Use the following steps for this process:

1. Taking each of the five changes, one at a time, ask participants by a show of hands to indicate whether they resisted the change, were leaders in adjusting to the change, or just went along with it. Record their responses on the easel pad.

2. Depending on the size of your group, select the change or changes that had the most evenly split response between those who resisted the change and those who supported it. Form small groups of resisters and other groups of supporters.

3. Allow each group up to 15 minutes to prepare arguments supporting their position, then have each small group in turn present these arguments to the total group. Conclude the session with a summary of the discussion.

3 Free to be you and me

People have very different lifestyles. As they plan for retirement, these varied patterns continue. A retirement lifestyle that is "right" for one person may be quite "wrong" for another. Individuals can design their own retirement; they can let others design it for them; or they can accept whatever comes along.

Objectives

To more clearly recognize the value of independent actions during retirement.

To choose to be engaged in society rather than disengaged.

To make the best possible choices among the retirement options available to us.

To recognize the value of making our own choices rather than allowing choices to be made for us by forces such as family, community, and finances.

Group size

10–30 participants.

Time

30–40 minutes.

Materials

Choices and changes worksheet and pencils.

Background information

- The person who is positively retired is more independent than dependent, more engaged in society than disengaged, more satisfied with retirement than dissatisfied, and freer to make their own choices than to be controlled by others.

- Adults most positive in their retirement are those who make changes as they go along. They have learned to adjust as situations change.

- Sometimes change is gradual, but at other times rapid change is required after a crisis.

Process

1. Introduce the exercise by presenting and elaborating briefly on the following information:

    - Most positive retirees are independent rather than dependent.
    - They are actively engaged in society.
    - They tend to be satisfied with their retirement lifestyle.
    - To a great extent, they are free to make their own decisions.

2. Distribute a copy of the **Choices and changes** worksheet to each participant and provide the following instructions:

    ➤ Ask yourself how independent you are right now. Financial security is only one aspect of this issue. Your independence may be restricted by poor physical or emotional health, by responsibilities to other people, or by some other factor. Turn to the first item on your **Choices and changes** worksheet and underline the number that indicates your current level of independence. Now ask yourself whether you are satisfied with that level of independence and circle the number that indicates the level you would prefer at this time in your life.

➤ Consider the second item on your worksheet and ask yourself whether you have a satisfying number of intimate relationships among family members and friends. Do you regularly spend time with these people, and do you also enjoy a variety of casual acquaintances? Underline the number that indicates your level of social engagement right now and circle the number that indicates the level you would prefer.

➤ Look at the third item on your worksheet. Do you feel generally satisfied or dissatisfied with your life? Does each day present new and interesting challenges, or at this time, do you tend to find little meaning in life? Underline the number that indicates your current level of satisfaction with life and circle the number that indicates the level you would prefer.

➤ Consider the fourth item on your worksheet. If we allow it to happen, our lives can be controlled by many things, including other people and social norms—even ones we don't really believe in. Underline the number that indicates to what extent you are free to live life as you choose. Now circle the number that indicates the level of freedom you would prefer.

➤ Complete the final questions on the worksheet.

3. Form groups of four to six participants and provide the following instructions:

➤ Select a recorder to take notes and report the ideas generated by your small group.

➤ Review your worksheets and discuss the following questions, attempting to develop practical solutions

©1997 Whole Person Press 210 W Michigan Duluth MN 55802   (800) 247-6789

for people who would like to make changes in their life. You will have 10 minutes for this activity.

✔ How can a person become more independent?

✔ How can a person become more socially engaged?

✔ How can a person find more satisfaction in retirement life?

✔ How can a person gain the freedom to control their own retirement destiny?

4. After 10 minutes, ask the reporters to come to the front of the room. As they present the ideas of their groups, moderate a discussion among the reporters, focusing on several of the best ideas.

5. Conclude the session by opening the discussion to questions or ideas from all participants.

Variations

Variations will be required if the group has fewer than fifteen or more than forty members.

- If the group has fewer than fifteen members, the small groups need not be formed. Begin the discussion following completion of the worksheet by individuals.

- If the group has more than forty participants, select half the reporters to discuss the first two items on the list. Then replace that group with the remaining reporters for discussion of the last two items. Control the time carefully in order to allow a few minutes for a closing discussion.

©1997 Whole Person Press 210 W Michigan Duluth MN 55802   (800) 247-6789

Choices and changes

Independence

1	2	3	4	5	6	7	8	9	10

Dependent   Independent

Social engagement

1	2	3	4	5	6	7	8	9	10

Socially disengaged   Socially engaged

Satisfaction with life

1	2	3	4	5	6	7	8	9	10

Dissatisfied   Satisfied

Freedom

1	2	3	4	5	6	7	8	9	10

Controlled by others   Free to be myself

In which area do you find the greatest difference between where you are now and where you would like to be? ____

_____

_____

What can you do to reduce that difference? _____

_____

_____

©1997 Whole Person Press 210 W Michigan Duluth MN 55802   (800) 247-6789

4   Life changes and choices

Personal choices, when delayed too long, become a barrier to a great retirement.

In this exercise, participants consider when specific decisions should be made in order for them to achieve the four broad objectives of independence, engagement, satisfaction, and freedom.

Objectives

To understand that we older adults often make choices much later than we should.

To become aware of the decisions that should be made early in life.

To be motivated to "catch up" on decisions that have been overlooked or delayed.

To look ahead and begin to make choices early.

To become more willing to confer with others about retirement planning.

Group size

Unlimited.

Time

30–40 minutes.

Materials

Timeline worksheet and pencils; easel pad and markers.

Process

1. Introduce the exercise by presenting a brief talk based on the following information:

- Planning for retirement is better done early in life rather than late.
- Most people wait too long to begin making retirement plans.
- The present cohort (age group) of retirees needs to plan for more retirement years than any previous group.
- Access to information on retirement is more available to this generation than to any previous group.

2. Distribute the **Timeline** worksheet to all participants and tell them that they will have the opportunity to examine the retirement choices they have made and those they have not yet made.

3. Draw a vertical line on the easel pad similar to that on the worksheet and, as you give the instructions below, follow the steps on the easel pad.

   ➤ On your worksheet, you will see a timeline like this one on the easel pad. It is divided by tens, indicating ages twenty to eighty. You will also find a numbered list of actions that should be taken in relation to retirement.

   ➤ Recall at what age you took each of these actions and, on the left side of the timeline, place the number of the action next to that age. If you have not yet taken the action, skip the item.

   ➤ Then consider at what age you believe you should have taken the action. On the right side of the time line, place the number of the action next to that age. You will have 10 minutes to complete the worksheet.

4. While participants are working, post signs numbered 20, 30 . . . 80 plus a sign labeled "not yet done" along one wall of the meeting room.

©1997 Whole Person Press 210 W Michigan Duluth MN 55802   (800) 247-6789

5. After participants have completed the worksheet, ask them to stand, then give the following instructions:

   ➤ As I read each action on the worksheet, move to the sign representing the age at which you took that action.

   ➤ Then move to the age at which you believe that action should be taken.

6. One at a time read each action and ask people to take the two steps listed above. Record the differences that you note between when people believe they should have done things and when they actually did them. When the difference is significant, pause for discussion and ask participants why they believe those specific choices were made.

   ☞ *If the group is so large that this movement is unwieldy, or if the time is too short, simply have people raise their hands in response to item. Ask a recorder to chart significant differences.*

7. When all actions have been read, ask people to return to their seats, then continue with a discussion of their observations.

8. Conclude by making the following summary comments.

   ■ Although there is no exact time at which choices about retirement should occur, there is a general period during which, if we make the choices, they will have the best chance of making a positive impact on our life after retirement.

   ■ If you have not yet made some of these choices, you may want to learn from the shared wisdom of those in our group who believe they should have made some of their decisions earlier.

   ■ You don't have to make your choices in a vacuum. A vast amount of information is available and easy to find. (You may want to list local sources of retirement information on a handout and make it available to participants.)

Variation

■ If the group comprises thirty or fewer participants, a discussion could replace steps 4–7. During the discussion, ask individuals to comment on why they made decisions too late and why certain decisions have been difficult to make.

Timeline

	Age action was taken	Age action should have been taken
1. First planned for Social Security and pension.		
2. Started systematic savings for retirement.	80	
3. Did comprehensive estate planning.		
4. Discussed retirement with family members.	70	
5. Chose a life purpose for retirement.		
6. Decided to be of service to others during retirement.	60	
7. Left employment in whole or in part.		
8. Sought new friendships for my retirement years.	50	
9. Made decisions on my will and living will.		
10. Began to drop some activities and start new ones.	40	
11. Examined my total health plan (physical, financial, attitudinal).		
12. Considered living arrangements (adapting to physical change, new interests).	30	
13. Chose to overcome barriers that curtailed freedom.		
14. Decided to seek a good life in retirement.	20	
15. Decided to use the wisdom that comes with age.		

5 Thinking retirement? A dialogue

Whether those approaching retirement have spent their careers in large organizations or in independent enterprises, they need to plan for the time they will leave their career. In either situation, it's important to make plans and decisions prior to leaving the world of work. Interviews with two people who are preparing for retirement will encourage participants to begin making these plans themselves.

Objectives

To see more clearly the variety of choices that early planning provides.

To relate directly and with more empathy to others struggling with decisions about retirement.

To ask some of the questions considered in the dialogue and to become more aware of resources that will be of direct help.

To find it easier to enter into discussions with others on some of the tougher questions about retirement planning.

Group size

Unlimited.

Time

40 minutes.

Materials

Planning assessment worksheet and pencils.

☞ *Prior to the session, select two persons nearing retirement who are willing to be interviewed during the session about any retirement planning they have or have not done. These interviewees may be selected from within the group or from the outside.*

To encourage a wide-ranging discussion, it is preferable that the two people you select have begun to think of planning but have yet to develop detailed plans. If possible select one man and one woman, one person whose career has been in a large organization such as industry, business, or government and one who has worked independently or in a small organization with few resources for retirement planning.

Process

1. Introduce the concept of retirement planning by presenting some of the following background information.

   ■ Persons working in large organizations usually have resources for retirement planning provided by employers; those working independently or in a small family business have fewer resources to call on.

   ■ Planning resources are available from community organizations and agencies including schools and colleges, agencies on aging, churches, AARP, and senior centers.

   ■ In the past, retirement planning programs focused almost exclusively on health and finance. Only recently have these programs included whole-person concepts, such as setting long-term goals for personal development, public service, part-time retirement careers, and continued learning.

2. Distribute the **Planning assessment** worksheet and provide the following instructions:

   ➤ This **Planning assessment** worksheet will give you the chance to evaluate whether or not you are making appropriate retirement plans in all areas of your life.

➤ After each item on the list, make a check in the appropriate column to indicate whether you have made no plans, some plans, or well-developed plans. You will have 5 minutes.

3. When everyone has finished the worksheet, introduce the selected interviewees and begin asking them the questions on the worksheet. Your challenge is to encourage the interviewees to be honest in their answers and to help them feel comfortable even if they have not yet made needed retirement plans. Questions in the variation section at the end of this exercise provide additional options that will encourage discussion.

4. Following the dialogue, conclude the exercise by asking participants to identify the ways in which this discussion may help them in their own retirement planning.

☞ *With some groups you may choose to use the variation before proceeding to the summary.*

Variation

■ Following the dialogue, summarize the group's worksheet responses. Prepare in advance by duplicating the worksheet on the easel pad.

Ask for a show of hands in response to each item on the worksheet and record the count on the easel pad.

When this survey is complete, use some of the following questions to encourage discussion.

✔ Health—What barriers have you discovered to health care planning? How can you get past these barriers?

✔ Financial—Have you determined: your tentative yearly budget? your annual income after retirement? your net worth? your investment strategy?

✔ Hobbies and leisure—Have you developed special skills? Do you have long-term interests? Do you own materials and equipment? Are you interested in individual or group activities?

✔ Travel—Do you want to visit any special places? Do you enjoy staying around home? Do you prefer extended or brief travel? Are you prepared to finance the traveling you wish to do?

✔ Continued learning—Do you have a backlog of community education or college classes you wish to take? Do you want to start any special self-directed learning projects? Do you prefer to enrich what you already know rather than to start something entirely new?

✔ Elderhostels—Do you receive the seasonal catalog? Have you looked at the catalogs in your library? Have you talked to folks who have attended Elderhostels?

✔ A retirement career—Do you have ideas about what you would like to do after you retire? Would you prefer a retirement career that earns money or one that is not salaried but makes your life worthwhile?

✔ Community service—Are you comfortable serving on boards and commissions? Is there a need for service to your church or to schools and other local organizations? Would you like to be involved in community development projects such as park improvement, cleanup campaigns, recycling, and local history?

✔ Caregiving—Would you prefer to focus on family or on the general community? Do you have special talents that are needed, such as the ability to work with young children or nursing home residents?

✔ Writing memoirs—Would you want to do this as a gift to your family? Because of interest in sharing your knowledge of the past? Because it will keep your brain cells active?

✔ Genealogy—Would you want to do this as a gift to your family? Because of interest in sharing your knowledge of the past? Because it will keep the brain cells active?

Planning assessment

Item	No plans	Some plans	Thorough plans
Health care			
Financial plan			
Hobbies and leisure			
Travel			
Continued learning			
Elderhostels			
Retirement career			
Community service			
Caregiving			
Write memoirs			
Genealogy			
List others			

Patterns of aging

6 Leaving the job and living free

In this exercise, participants will anticipate and share the adventures that come with leaving their jobs and planning the next twenty years.

Previous generations missed the opportunity we have to switch from the responsibilities of an eight-hour workday to the freedom of twenty-four hours in which we can do as we choose.

We need to be as imaginative and as venturesome about this new freedom as when we were teenagers and had unlimited choices about what to do with our lives.

Objectives

To be able more openly to express feelings and concerns about retirement and plans for the future.

To clarify the intangible benefits of work that must be compensated for with informed freedom of choice and self-direction.

Group size

25 or fewer is preferable.

Time

1-$\frac{1}{2}$ hours.

Materials

Two name tags for each participant; easel pad and markers.

Process

1. Introduce the concept that retiring from a career presents both an ending and a beginning. Retirement will produce mixed feelings, apprehension at times and joy

and anticipation at other times. Over and above the paycheck, our work gives many intangible benefits:

- Identity: Whether we are doctors, secretaries, teachers, electricians, or clerks, people identify us by the work we do. Most retirees, therefore, need to build a new identity. This is especially true if we move to a different community upon retirement.

- Schedule: For most of us, our career mandated our daily schedule. After retirement, we must provide a structure that gives meaning to our days.

- Productiveness: During our working years, our jobs provided us with feelings of productivity. Now we must face the fact that, for our own well-being, we must feel satisfied that we are contributing members of society. We need to feel good about being givers, not takers.

- Challenge: A job usually pushes us to keep learning and adapting. It stimulates us mentally, physically, and often emotionally. To keep all our systems in running order—body, mind, beliefs, values, emotions, and appreciations, we still need to be challenged.

- People: Our job was a place where we found friends. As our lives change, we need to keep on making and cultivating friendships.

2. Divide participants into groups of four and then distribute two blank name tags to each person with the following instructions:

> Fill out the first name tag in a way that would introduce you to a group of people you don't know. On this card, print information that would identify you one year before your retirement.

> Fill out the second name tag in the same manner,

©1997 Whole Person Press 210 W Michigan Duluth MN 55802   (800) 247-6789

except on it print information that would identify you one year after your retirement.

3. After participants have completed their name tags, ask each person in the small group to read their two introductions to the other three participants. Encourage members of each group to make suggestions on how to build a new identity as a retiree.

4. Reconvene the group and ask members of each group to share their insights. Record on the easel pad the most helpful suggestions from each group.

5. Lead a discussion on how to build a new identity after retirement, building on the group's suggestions and on some of the questions listed below.

✔ Does loss of status occur for some people when they retire?

✔ Should titles such as doctor, professor, judge, etc. be retained by the retiree?

✔ What is the best way to build your identity in a new community?

✔ Consider the following introduction: "I'd like you to meet my friend Joe. He was a manager at Cadley Brothers." What is wrong with this kind of an introduction? When could this kind of introduction be useful?

6. As an introduction to the story that follows, list on the easel pad the benefits of a career that were previously described:

■ the schedule it imposed on us

■ the sense of productiveness it gave us

■ the mind stretching and learning it required

■ the challenges it made us meet

■ the friendships it brought into our life

7. Read aloud the story that begins on page 31, **It's yours for the choosing,** to illustrate how retirement can sometimes bring the realization that the benefits of a career are missing in retirement and must be replaced for retirement to be successful.

8. After the story has been read, use the following questions as a discussion guide:

   ✔ Ross was left without a schedule and experienced a loss of purpose in his life. What are some examples from your own experience or from the experiences of people you know that helped lead you or someone else out of this initial loss into a schedule with purpose?

   ✔ How can a new retiree discover a retirement career, paid or unpaid, that is new and challenging?

   ✔ What "desires" or "causes" have you intended to pursue when you retire? How would you go about finding opportunities to begin with them?

Variation

■ This session can be used in several ways. If a single session is scheduled for one hour or a bit longer, then a short break should be planned between steps 6 and 7. If planned for two 30–40 minute sessions, begin the second session with step 7. The two-session plan would work best with clubs or church groups accustomed to 30-minute programs.

It's yours for the choosing

Two recent retirees, Ross McNulty and Clyde Gill, were lunching at the Tipler Hills Golf Club at Ross's request. Ross had phoned Clyde, pushed by a feeling of desperation and boredom. It was six months since his retirement bash. He was sick to death of TV, cutting grass, playing golf, and fishing. Several times he said to himself, "This is hell, I hate it!"

Ross had a specific question to ask, and it came as they awaited their sandwiches and coffee—"What in heaven's name do you do with yourself now that you're retired, Clyde? I've only been out six months, and I'm sick of the whole thing."

Clyde looked startled. They'd worked together at First Federal Savings and Loan for years. Both were money management experts at the executive level, highly skilled and competent. "Ross, I'm surprised to hear you say that. I thought you were eager to be free of the load of responsibility."

Ross frowned, "I thought I was. But now I can't seem to find the energy or enthusiasm for anything. I'm bored to death. I want to know what you are doing these days."

"Well, honestly, I'm having a ball, Ross. Although I hate to put it like that because it sounds a bit 'holier than thou.' Let me summarize a bit. Looking back, I did go through a short period of feeling the way you describe. I found out very soon that I couldn't just play golf and putter around the house and yard all of the time."

"You're not working again part-time, are you?"

"Not for pay, but yes, I'm working on some things I feel are important enough to give my time and effort to. For one thing, I took on the job of treasurer of my church. They sure needed help from someone who knew how to keep books and give financial advice. Now I'm on the church board, and I find that I enjoy the people I work with immensely. Then Annie and I both are interested in antiques. We have great fun going to auctions, and I've ended up with a furniture refinishing hobby that won't quit. I've even placed a few finished pieces at Rutherfords and two have been sold."

"Time doesn't hang heavy on your hands?" Ross asked.

"On the contrary, I'm too busy, and everything I do, I want to do. Annie and I have each taken a few special classes, such as art history, and we've both taken one on refinishing furniture. Met a lot of folks just as nutty about antiques as we are. We've even gone to three Elderhostel programs with art and philosophy as a focus. There's a whole world of opportunity waiting for you, Ross. It's yours for the choosing."

Later, reporting the conversation to his wife, Mary, Ross said, "I have to admit that I've been bored lately. How would you feel if I started a little consulting business right here at the house? I think I need some work to do."

But Ross didn't start it because the very next morning he saw this announcement in the morning paper:

County Administrator Announces New Position

Elizabeth Barton, County Administrator, announces approval of a new quarter-time position in the County Aging Office. The position is in financial planning and statistical research. The developing programs for older adults in the county have demonstrated the need for this kind of expertise, Ms. Barton said. She also stated that the County Board prefers to employ a retiree from the financial community.

Ross applied, got the job, and became part of an exciting new County Service Program.

©1997 Whole Person Press 210 W Michigan Duluth MN 55802   (800) 247-6789

7   Retirement careers: activity with purpose

Retirees continue to need the satisfaction of accomplishment and productive work. This exercise describes a wide variety of purposeful activities open to elders; it also shows the diversity of interests in a group of older adults.

Out of 140 elders identified as models of positive retirement, fewer than ten were employed for pay, but all were working to achieve some purpose. The writers have chosen to call such purposes "retirement careers."

Objectives

To understand that existing talents, skills, and knowledge as well as new skills and interests can be used productively by retirees.

To appreciate that having a cause is stimulating and invigorating.

To realize that we need not try to do everything; rather we need to choose those activities that we do well and that bring us the greatest satisfaction.

Group size

10–30 participants is optimum. In larger groups of up to 60 participants, more discussion would have to be done in the small groups.

Time

60–90 minutes.

Materials

Retirement career cards; easel pad and markers; paper and pencils.

Process

1. Introduce the exercise by making the following points:

   ■ Retirees are a rich resource for their communities when they willingly take on productive roles which cry out for leadership and work.

   ■ Conversely, retirees themselves need purposeful activity for health and for life satisfaction. Donald Super, an expert in career development gives us this definition of career—"the course of events which constitute a life; the sequence of occupations and life roles which combine to express one's own commitment to work in his or her total pattern of self-development."

   ■ Simply put, a retirement career is a strong commitment to use one's talent, knowledge, and energy in an area where help is needed. These areas include the arts, business, community service, political action, historic preservation, church, and service organizations, among others.

2. Read the following example of one couple who developed this concept in the community to which they moved for retirement.

   Mary and Joe Stevens retired in their mid-fifties, full of energy and enthusiastic about making this a great time in their lives. Mary developed her ceramics hobby into a small business with Joe as chief assistant. Their winter vacations were trips to Opryland, with an additional week spent in Mississippi helping at Habitat for Humanity. Mary, who had worked extensively with office equipment before retirement, took on the task of editing and typing their church newsletter. Joe volunteered to serve as a member of the Cook County Hospital Board, which was planning a large addition. Thus their retirement careers encompass business, volunteer work, and community service.

3. Form groups of four to six people and distribute paper

©1997 Whole Person Press 210 W Michigan Duluth MN 55802   (800) 247-6789

and pencils. Give the following directions allowing 5 minutes for participants to complete their task:

➤ Write a short description of a retiree you personally know who has an interesting retirement career either for pay or as a volunteer.

➤ Briefly describe a developed or undeveloped talent you have and would like to explore.

4. After 5 minutes, encourage participants to share their examples with others in their group.

5. Distribute a set of the **Retirement career cards** to each participant in each group. Read the title of each card and offer a real-life example such as the ones listed below for each of the twelve areas of retirement career choices.

Careers in the arts: Ade Tofte, a retired newspaper editor in Cook County, Minnesota, transformed his garage into a studio and painted landscapes for pleasure and for income.

Careers in lifelong learning: Jeanne Mahony, a handicapped retiree, delved deeply into the history of her town and, working with others, established a prize-winning local folk museum in Mazomanie, Wisconsin.

Careers in volunteer services: Vi Nelson began a program of reading aloud every Wednesday morning to a group at the nursing home in Grand Marais, Minnesota. Other volunteers heard about it and organized parties to celebrate special occasions.

Hobbies and special skills as retirement careers: Gertrude and Louis Zander, working as a team, focused on antiques. Gertrude spotted potentially beautiful antiques at sales, and Louis, an excellent carpenter, restored them. They cooperated on the finishing process.

Careers serving churches and organizations: Bev Gruman, a newcomer in Grand Marais when she and her husband retired there, joined the Garden Club and, using her expertise with flowers, volunteered to manage the Memorial Rose Garden and plant flowers at the county health clinic.

Careers in community and politics: Author Doris and her daughter, Karen Neal, went to the Cook County Board and volunteered, if they could use the county fairgrounds building for a recycling center, to help get recycling started in the county. The board agreed; the program got community support; and three years later the board built and staffed a recycling center.

Careers in health concerns: Joyce Swanson, a "Befriender" in her church, took a special class on caring for Alzheimer's patients. Working with others, she spent time almost every Friday providing companionship and outings for a woman diagnosed with Alzheimer's.

Careers in aid of a cause: Frank Gillis, emeritus professor of music, was president of the Library Friends when $20,000 in contributions were needed to buy the site for a new library. In a county of just 4,000 people this was no small task. Frank led the "house to house" campaign to raise the money. With the help he generated, the goal was reached, and the new library was constructed.

Careers in business and finance: Ray and Virginia Quick transformed a small bookstore in Grand Marais into The Book Station, a shop that specializes in books about the local area and Indian lore along with locally produced art and craft items.

Family-centered careers: Author Burt began searching for others with the same family name living throughout the United States. He discovered they all traced

©1997 Whole Person Press 210 W Michigan Duluth MN 55802   (800) 247-6789

their family name to a local area in Prussia. There were four strands of immigrants from the same area, but thus far he has found no direct tie among the strands. An annual letter continues in a search for this tie.

Careers as a special activities leader: The pastor's wife at Bethlehem Lutheran Church in Grand Marais started a book club for women of the church and their friends. After fifteen years, the members still gather every other Tuesday morning for stimulating reviews and lively discussions.

Careers in recreational skill development: Avid tennis enthusiasts Frances and Gordon Jarchow retired to Cook County where few people played tennis. Within two years the Jarchows helped spark a tennis organization, tennis tournaments, and a youth program.

6. After reading the career examples, ask participants if they have any questions about any of the twelve career areas. After addressing any of the questions, give participants the following instructions:

> ➤ Look over the twelve areas of the **Retirement career cards** and place the three that are of highest interest to you in rank order. These should be the ones you most enjoy or believe you would find most satisfying.

> ➤ After everyone in the group has made their selection, one at a time, report the three areas you chose and give a one-sentence reason for your choice. You will have 15 minutes total for this process.

> ➤ Select a recorder for your group to keep track of the areas that each person selected and to note interesting reasons for those selections.

7. After about 15 minutes, reconvene the entire group and ask each group's recorder to report the three most

frequently chosen areas and the key reasons given in their group for those selections.

8. Lead a discussion about the retirement career areas most frequently chosen, using some of the following questions:

✔ Is it necessary to earn financial rewards to get satisfaction from a retirement career in the arts?

✔ To take on a job or to run a business means a sacrifice of freedom. How can you keep at least part of your freedom?

✔ At age sixty, is it too late to get a college degree? How could you do it?

✔ How could you get a few people to join you in starting an exercise group, for example, a hiking group?

✔ Church pastors are always in need of assistants for visiting members who are ill. What kind of training might be needed to help with this?

✔ Can you compel children and grandchildren to attend family gatherings? If not, how can these events be made enjoyable for younger people?

✔ In what areas of city or county government would you like to see changes made? How can you get the attention of policy makers?

✔ How might you help get a recycling program started?

✔ What could you do to make your senior center a more stimulating place for younger retirees?

✔ Schools today draw much criticism. How can elders help our schools?

✔ While skills and hobbies are basically personal, how can we share them?

✔ Bridge is a stimulating mental activity. How could you use this game to benefit yourself and others?

9. In conclusion, make the following comments and ask participants who agree with the statements for supportive comments.

- Retirement is a time to develop those talents you may have neglected.

- The great benefit from working for others is what it does for us.

- If we are pushing ourselves to learn new things we are moving forward.

Variation

- This exercise could be split into two sessions. Conclude the first session after step 4 by reconvening the groups and asking participants to report examples of interesting retirement careers and share some of their own talents. Then distribute the **Retirement career cards** and continue through steps 5 and 6, asking participants to review and rank the cards prior to the next session.

Retirement career cards

Retirement careers in the arts

Fine arts: painting, sculpture
Craft arts: weaving, wood carving, ceramics, pottery
Music: instrumental, vocal
Theater: acting, producing, set design, costumes
Writing: poetry, fiction, nonfiction, journalism

Activities: produce, perform, teach

Retirement careers in lifelong learning

Independent study
Adult community education
Literacy, high school, GED, vocational, college
Travel, Elderhostels

Activities: teach or learn, start a study group or investment club, lead a travel group, organize a community forum, study local history, pursue a hobby

Retirement careers in volunteer service

RSVP and other formal volunteer programs
Senior centers, nursing homes, libraries
School helpers and mentors, foster grandparents
Docents in museums, galleries, and historic sites

Activities: chauffeur older adults, assist with office work, drive for Meals on Wheels, lead programs and parties, mentor children with learning problems

Retirement career cards

Hobbies and special skills as retirement careers

Rock collecting and polishing
Carpentry, antique restoration
Needlepoint, embroidery, knitting, crocheting
Fashion sewing, quilting

Activities: produce, teach, build a skill

Retirement careers serving churches & organizations
Board member, policy and decision maker
Officer
Organizer, fund-raiser
Loyal and hard-working member
Teacher, historian, publicist

Activities: accept a leadership role, be a committed
working member, assist with outreach, use your talents

Retirement careers in community & politics
Run for office: local, city, county
Serve on an appointed board or commission
Organize a group to bring specific proposals to boards
    or councils when needs arise

Activities: serve on hospital, library, planning, zoning, or
waste management boards; attend open meetings; study
local political issues; write letters; publicize programs

©1997 Whole Person Press 210 W Michigan Duluth MN 55802   (800) 247-6789

Retirement career cards

Retirement careers in health concerns

Encourage exercise among community elders
Work with health promotion groups
Work with county health nurse at a senior center
Begin drives for community swimming pool, safe hiking
    trail, senior exercise center, etc.

Activities: organize a support group, lead an exercise
group, help shut-ins

Retirement careers in aid of a cause

Environmental, safety
Political
Financial in support of a cause
Peace, justice, antidiscrimination
Youth and family, women's rights

Activities: lobby decision makers, speak to groups,
write articles for the newspaper, build a coalition

Retirement careers in business and finance

Study economic trends and investments
Work full- or part-time in a local business
Start a small business or contribute your skills to others
Work in a tourist information center of a state park
Help seniors with their tax returns

Activities: sales person, manager, cashier, host or host-
ess, business owner, chamber of commerce worker

Retirement career cards

Retirement careers focused on family

Caregiver, give care to or raise a grandchild
Executor of an estate
Genealogist or family historian
Counselor or support giver
The hub—holding the generations together

Activities: provide family gathering place, pass on traditions, be a listener, provide respite or long-term care

---

Retirement careers as a special activities leader

Program chairperson for an organization
Program organizer for senior center
Travel group or Elderhostel planner
Organizer—book club, bridge, chess, checkers, cribbage
Form theater or concert groups to attend performances

Activities: plan stimulating recreational, travel, and other programs for yourself and others

---

Retirement careers in recreational skill development

Bridge, tennis, golf
Swimming
Skiing, hiking
Computer use and Internet
Informal writing or poetry group

Activities: develop skills through learning and practice, teach skills to others, support ethical standards

---

©1997 Whole Person Press 210 W Michigan Duluth MN 55802   (800) 247-6789

8 A partnership that flourishes in retirement

Retirement can be the happiest, most stimulating, and most satisfying period in a relationship. This exercise will encourage people who are living with a partner to understand that in retirement their partnership can be enhanced and deepened.

Objectives

To recognize the need for couples to make major long-term plans together, considering the interests of both partners.

To make decisions appropriate to our own cohort (age group) rather than copying patterns of previous generations.

To recognize each other's views and to accept differences.

To build on the differences between partners so that both may be enriched.

To understand that a special objective for some older women is expanding their horizons beyond home and church.

Group size

20–40 is ideal. The closer to an equal number of men and women, the better.

Time

30–40 minutes, longer for a large group.

Materials

Easel pad and markers; paper and pencils.

Process

1. Introduce the exercise by making the following comments:

©1997 Whole Person Press 210 W Michigan Duluth MN 55802   (800) 247-6789

- Retirees have more togetherness than at any time since their honeymoon. They have an opportunity to make a fulfilling life together.

- However, if togetherness unveils differences in interests that were previously only suspected, differences that affect where to live, how to live, and how to spend time, retirement can be a time of dissension and escalating conflict.

2. On the easel pad, list the following scenarios, then give participants 3 minutes to select the one they find most interesting and to devise a plan that, despite their divergent interests, could satisfy both partners.

- The homebody wife and her world-traveler husband.

- The scholarly husband and his party-loving wife.

- The year-round golfer and his shy poet wife.

- The retired county executive wife and her carpentry-crafts husband.

3. One at a time, introduce each scenario and ask for ideas and discussion. Remind participants that each of the partner's interests and talents must be included in planning. The following suggestions may be offered if the group has difficulty developing solutions.

- The homebody wife and the world traveler husband might find that they can happily travel together if they create a comfortable home away from home in a rented apartment or condo, then spend a month or more thoroughly exploring the surrounding area.

- The scholarly husband needs a place of retreat in the retirement home. His party-loving wife will undoubtedly find her place in several community organizations. She should only insist on her husband's attendance at parties that include others with intellectual interests and opportunities for scintillating conversation.

©1997 Whole Person Press 210 W Michigan Duluth MN 55802   (800) 247-6789

- The year-round golfer will want to follow the sun south in winter so he can play all year, but a vacation home in a warm sunny place that also provides beauty and serenity can provide inspiration and enjoyment for his poet wife as well.

- The capable and motivated executive wife will undoubtedly soon chair several committees. To keep from growing apart, this couple, like many others, needs to find some new common interests that they can enjoy together.

4. Conclude this discussion by making the following points:

- Each member of a partnership needs to give space and encouragement to the other to develop and enhance individual as well as common interests. Unless the couple grows together, they will grow apart. For those who prior to retirement have solved this challenge, retirement will be a snap!

- During retirement, we can continue to grow by using our talents and by developing special interests. Each person needs the freedom to keep on developing both as an individual and as a member of a partnership.

5. Introduce and expand on the concept of a cohort with the following comments:

- Age-group cohorts include those people who were born within approximately a ten-year period. People in their seventies are somewhat different from those in their sixties because they had different experiences during their formative years. Present seventy-year-olds were adolescents during the Depression and were of military age during World War II. Present sixty-year-olds were adolescents during that war and enjoyed prosperity in their young adulthood.

- In the present cohort of older adults, most women

were homemakers and men were wage earners. But a dramatic change occurred for the Baby Boomer generation. Most women among these couples will have been wage earners, and their husbands will have probably helped with homemaking.

- For some couples today, times of retirement no longer coincide. One partner may retire many years before the other is ready to do so.

- New family structures have also emerged among younger retirees. Family groups often include his kids, her kids, and our kids.

- Because life spans have increased dramatically during the twentieth century, careful, long-range retirement planning has become essential. Life expectancies for both men and women have increased by nearly ten years.

6. For the small-group discussion, divide the two cohort groups (pre- and post-retirement) by gender, forming four groups, made up as follows:

Cohort 1—women 65 and older

Cohort 2—women 64 and younger

Cohort 3—men 65 and older

Cohort 4—men 64 and younger

> ☞ *If your participants include only men or only women or if they are present in very unequal numbers, form small groups in the most logical way.*

7. Distribute paper and pencils and assign each group the following tasks, allowing 10 minutes to complete them:

➤ List up to five special personal interests you spend time on or wish to spend time on during retirement.

➤ List two special ambitions (secret ambitions, perhaps)

that you have never been able to do successfully or have never had the freedom to tackle.

➤ Determine ways in which your partner could help you reach the personal ambitions that you listed above.

8. When everyone has completed the task, allow 5 minutes for participants to share their responses within the group. Encourage them to choose two responses to be shared with the other groups.

9. Reconvene the total group and ask each group to state their cohort's identity (i.e. women 65 and older) and share the responses they selected.

10. Conclude the session with a short discussion based on one or more of the following questions:

✔ Can you offer an example of how sharing interests or encouraging a partner's special interest brought a positive dimension to retirement?

✔ Can you recall a situation in which a couple's refusal to share interests led them to draw apart from each other?

✔ Are you aware of situations in which one partner refused to allow the other to pursue a special interest? In what ways did this affect their relationship?

✔ How different is retirement for partners who both had employment careers and for partners only one of whom had an employment career?

✔ What can organizations (church, clubs, senior centers, and others) do to get partners to share retirement goals and activities?

9 You and your friends

People need people. It is a universal truth that we need family, acquaintances, neighbors, colleagues, and friends to fulfill our basic needs as human beings.

Objectives

To recognize that making new friends and using social skills is important at any age, but becomes even more crucial as we age.

To identify the levels of social interaction that lead to friendship.

To practice, better understand, and use the social skill of conversation.

Group size

Best for 10–30 people.

Time

45–60 minutes.

Materials

Easel pad and markers; paper and pencils; a photocopy of each of the **Three levels of friendly interaction** cards.

Process

1. Introduce the session with the following comments:
   - People need people—family, acquaintances, neighbors, colleagues, and friends.
   - Elders need to keep making new friends to replace those taken from them by relocation, illness, and death.

©1997 Whole Person Press 210 W Michigan Duluth MN 55802   (800) 247-6789

- We know that friends are a vital part of our life. Psychologist Abraham Maslow gives us a good explanation of why this is true.

2. Copy the Maslow Pyramid of Human Needs on the easel pad as you explain it.

- Everyone recognizes that the bottom two levels of this pyramid represent the bare essentials for life.
- The top three levels, which represent psychological needs, must be met for us to live a satisfying and meaningful life. Those needs can only be met in relationships with other people.

3. Form three groups by having participants count off by threes. After they have moved into their groups, introduce the next activity.

- Friendly interactions with people occur at different levels of meaning, but all friendships are important to our well-being.
- Think of a time when a friend made a crucial difference in your life and briefly relate the story to your group. You will have 10 minutes total for this activity.

4. After 10 minutes, distribute one of the **Three Levels of Friendly Interaction** cards to each group. Ask a person from Group 1 to read to the entire group the "Companionship level;" a person from Group 2, to read the "True communication level;" and a person from Group 3, to read the "Compassionate level."

5. Give each small group 10–15 minutes to prepare a short play that illustrates the level of friendly interaction assigned to them. They might look for inspiration to the friendly actions recalled by participants a few minutes earlier. The plays should be a conversation between two people. A third person can set the scene and present a summary statement at the end of the play.

6. After preparation, reconvene the entire group and have the small groups perform their plays. After each play ask for comments or personal thoughts generated by the plays.

7. Conclude the session with a discussion built on the following questions:

✔ Is it possible to establish true communication with everyone? Is it desirable?

✔ What strategies might you use to establish true communication with people who find it hard "to be themselves?"

✔ What are the rules about giving advice?

✔ What organizations or groups do you belong to that encourage you to be a friend?

✔ What are some of the special actions which promote friendship?

☞ *Record these actions on the easel pad as they are mentioned.*

Three levels of friendly interaction

The companionship level of interaction

Companions are pleasant and outgoing. Often they are the people who speak first, setting others at ease.

Example: Flo says her special talent is "being pleasant." In addition, she has a gift of comedy that spreads good humor wherever she goes. Flo loves the job of serving coffee at her senior center. In making the rounds, she teases and makes a bit of fun. "I get so much pleasure out of people," she says.

This companionship level makes no great demands on our time or effort. It only requires that we step beyond the barriers of self-consciousness.

The true communication level of interaction

True communication allows people to get beyond conversational pleasantries to talk about something they both care about. Instead of "Isn't it a beautiful day," one might say, "I was proud of you for speaking up at the Lion's Meeting last night. What you said was needed." True communication requires being totally open to speaking and to listening.

Example: Emma and her husband own a small grocery store in a low-income neighborhood. Emma runs the store on her own because her husband serves on the city council. Emma describes her friendly interaction with neighborhood women in this way: "Caring, sharing, and giving. I serve as a safety-valve for people to let off steam!" Emma says she has learned to keep confidences and withhold judgment.

To be a true communicator, be yourself, let down your barriers, and really listen to the other person.

©1997 Whole Person Press 210 W Michigan Duluth MN 55802   (800) 247-6789

Three levels of friendly interaction

The compassionate level of interaction

Compassionate people are willing to intervene on a friend's behalf or to minister to the needs of others. This is the most fulfilling level of friendly interaction. Psychologist Carl Rogers describes it as "being fully human. Fully to be a human being is to enter into the complex process of being one of the most widely sensitive, responsive, creative, and adaptive creatures on the planet."

Example: Anne, a sixty-eight-year-old widow, lives in a federally funded high-rise for senior citizens. She is a gentle, outgoing person who radiates warmth and concern. Although not paid to do so, Anne has taken on the task of checking on fellow residents who are ill. "If I know someone is ill behind a door, I make straight for that door." She explains her commitment like this. "When I was a child, I saw so much poverty and people on their own with no one to care for them that it must have gone deep inside my consciousness. When my husband died, it came to me that this is something I could do."

When people engage in the compassionate level of interaction, they approach the highest level on the Pyramid of Human Needs—self-actualization.

©1997 Whole Person Press 210 W Michigan Duluth MN 55802   (800) 247-6789

10 You and your family

For many of us, family ties are the most important relationships in our life. Although styles differ from culture to culture, family bonds connect the generations.

Objectives

To recognize the impact of change on family members.

To understand ways in which family members may encourage retirees to reexamine their goals.

To suggest ways that individuals, churches, and community organizations can help families adjust to retirement.

To objectively evaluate our own contributions to a positive retirement for ourselves and for others.

Group size

Works well with up to 50.

Time

40–50 minutes.

Materials

Easel pad and markers.

Process

1. Introduce the exercise by presenting some of the information below about how change affects American families.

   ■ Family is important from childhood through retirement.

   ■ As people progress through their life span, family relationships must change.

   ■ Children who learned to defer to their parents in all

©1997 Whole Person Press 210 W Michigan Duluth MN 55802   (800) 247-6789

things will be in trouble when they marry if that deference to parents continues.

- When families move to a new culture, parents often hold vigorously to their previous culture while their children adapt and often accept without question new beliefs and patterns of behavior.

- The role reversal that follows when, because of illness, parents require care from their children can be difficult for both.

2. Remind participants that some changes have their greatest impact on the marriage, others on the children, and still others on the relationships between the generations. As you list some of the family changes that require choices and adjustments, write them on the easel pad.

- Marriage, divorce, and remarriage

- Children

- Loss of job or job change requiring a geographic move

- Middle-age children moving back in with parents

- Elders' dependence on their children

- Severe illness

- Death

3. Ask participants to volunteer their ideas on other factors responsible for changes in the family. As they do so, add these ideas to the list on the easel pad.

4. Introduce the true story **Is Mother having an affair?** which is printed at the end of this exercise, by noting that the role reversals that sometimes come as people age can be confusing and difficult for parents as well as for their children. Ask participants to consider this as they listen to the story.

    ☞ *This story can be presented even more effectively by a group of four readers taking the parts of Grace, Ben,*

> *Wanda, and a narrator. The readers will need time for preparation.*

5. Read the story expressively. At its conclusion, ask participants the following questions, allowing time for at least three responses to each question.

   ✔ In this story, Jenny was helped directly by Wanda and indirectly by Grace and Ben. Should we, as friends and family members, be involved in attempts to lead negative retirees toward a more positive retirement?

   ✔ How can leaders and professionals in organizations such as senior centers, churches, and clubs design programs to accomplish that goal?

   ✔ If you received a call from your mother's doctor asking how best to inform your mother that her heart was deteriorating rapidly, what would you advise?

   ✔ If you were told that your own heart was deteriorating, would you try to change your lifestyle in any way?

   ✔ What should the role of family be in informing and educating older family members on how to deal with health problems?

   ✔ If you learned that your mother was having an affair, what would you do?

   ✔ If you were asked by your son or daughter, "How does your friend fit into your long-term plans? Am I going to have a stepparent?" how would you answer?

6. Form groups of eight to ten persons and give the following instructions:

   ➤ In your group, brainstorm ideas on how organizations such as churches, service clubs, and senior citizen centers can help establish an interchange among family members that will lead to a more positive retirement for many people.

➤ Select one of the ideas to report to the larger group.

7. Reconvene the group and ask representatives of the small groups to report their ideas. Summarize the ways in which community organizations can support retirees and their families.

Variation

■ The questions in step 5 could be organized into a role-playing setting. Assign one member of the group to play Grace and one to play the role of Jenny. Grace asks the question, and Jenny responds. Allow 5 minutes for the discussion.

©1997 Whole Person Press 210 W Michigan Duluth MN 55802   (800) 247-6789

Is Mother having an affair?

"I'm worried about Mother," Grace said to her husband, Ben. She had received another dismal letter from her mother, Jenny Abbott. Grace continued, "All she does is complain. She doesn't like to sit around the house; she can't tolerate visiting my brothers and sisters; and I know that she dislikes being here for more than a day or two. Listen to this postscript at the end of the letter. 'I know that I shouldn't write this to you, but if this is old age, I wish that I had been taken when your father was.'" Grace folded her mother's letter and turned to her husband.

Ben's response was to the point. "Your mother has never faced up to her problems. She is capable enough to do most anything if she would try. My Mom does more with her pacemaker than yours does with a sound heart."

Grace agreed. "Mom's life was her family, especially when the four of us were kids. I think she did a great job in those years. Her problems began when we left the nest. And since Dad died, it has been worse—not at all like your mother who seems to thrive on adversity. I'll bet that she cheered when you left home."

Ben nodded. "I know she did. Dad had been gone five years by then. Can you imagine being left with two teenage sons? When she started running around after Dad died, my brother and I were sure that she was dating. Later we realized that rejoining the Sweet Adelines and the church choir was what she had wanted to do for years. She preferred that to carting us around for all of our activities. We didn't blame her."

Grace responded with admission. "My mother wasn't a bit like Wanda, your mom. Mine has always left me confused. When we left home for college she wanted us back every vacation and then cried when we left for campus in the fall. It was always the same story of 'the house' being so lonesome. Remember the summer of our junior year when we did the Europe trek? She never forgave me for that. I felt guilty for not being home. In fact, Ben, that was the reason I agreed to marry during our senior year. I didn't want to spend another summer with her."

Ben had been thinking about what they might do to help, so he agreed at once when Grace suggested that they invite both Wanda and Jenny to spend Thanksgiving weekend with them.

Should they or should they not tell Wanda that they thought Jenny needed help? They considered this for a long time, even after the invitations were accepted. Finally Grace said she was going to phone her mother-in-law and tell her about her mother's problems.

Wanda went for the challenge. "Sure I'll try. It may not do much good but my volunteer counseling at the medical center has given me the skills to get through to people who always look for the worst during their recovery. You know, for some, the recovery from children leaving home or the loss of a spouse is just as trying as recovering from cancer or a heart attack. Some folks recover faster than others. If you think that your mom needs help, leave it to me. But please give us some time alone after Thanksgiving. Take the kids to the zoo or something. Stay away a good long time."

That response was what Ben expected. "Give Mom a challenge, and she takes it. You know, Grace, I finally believe her when she says that she learned how to handle anything during the hard times of the 1930s. Remember five years ago when she had her pacemaker put in? She didn't let us know until the night before so there was no time to feel sorry for her."

Ben and Grace learned little of the conversation that Wanda

and Jenny had over Thanksgiving, but after the Christmas holiday season, a letter came from Wanda. Grace read it to Ben. The last paragraph said that she would be staying with Jenny several days in late January. This would follow a Senior Citizen Sing in one of Chapel Hill's churches. Jenny would attend and pick Wanda up after the program.

Grace's reaction to this news was, "Wow! Mother has never gone to anything like this before. Maybe it's working."

There was a postscript to the letter. "After this, Jenny is going to have to get going on her own. I'm leaving my Elderhostel announcement with her, and I will underline several good ones I've attended or heard about. I will also tell her about the one on Vancouver Island that I will attend next summer. Truly, Jenny has been a challenge, but I do like her. The rest is up to her. Except, perhaps you, Grace, can encourage her to do more."

Then in February another letter arrived. In it they read, "If Jenny tells you about a date sometime this winter, don't be surprised. I ran into my old friend, Jim Walker, a widower, at the Senior Citizen Sing and introduced him to Jenny. He asked me out, but I agreed only after he promised to call Jenny for one of the spring concerts. Jenny needs someone in her life more than I do. She centered her life around her family for so many years that a good man may break through her inertia. Remember, you asked me to meddle!"

(one year later)

Wanda is still as involved as ever in a fine balance of activities that make for a positive retirement. Physical problems do not stop her. She chooses to do both service projects and fun things for herself. Her good deeds continue to spill over to others. She has strong commitments, is independent, has many friends, takes adult classes, and always looks forward to the next day. Her pacemaker slowed in midyear, so it was replaced by one going eighty-five beats per minute. Ben suggested that racing stripes be added if it ever again needs replacing.

Jenny is not Wanda, but what a change a year makes! Jenny now writes about things she is doing, not about what she cannot do. Grace never knew how much her mother enjoyed music and theater. Instead of a letter each week, the letters now arrive monthly, and they are shorter and shorter. Her March letter ended with , "Sorry, no time for anything else right now. A longer letter next time."

The next letter puzzled Grace. It closed with this line, "I know that you kids stop in unexpectedly sometimes, and I welcome your visits, but please let me know before you come."

Ben and Grace wondered aloud, "Is Mother having an affair?"

©1997 Whole Person Press 210 W Michigan Duluth MN 55802   (800) 247-6789

11 What is best for you?

Thinking for yourself is essential to achieving a great retirement. So is listening to what others think. The best answers result from systematically looking at your own knowledge, theories, and hunches about retirement and examining the knowledge, theories, and hunches of others who know you well, know retirement well, or both.

In this exercise participants are asked to make personal judgments on a series of simple statements that have no right or wrong answers. Differences will be noted, and alternative ways of responding will be identified.

Objectives

To have a more complete understanding of the retirement views of peers.

To be more objective in understanding why we respond and make judgments as we do.

To avoid making premature decisions that need further consideration and to carefully consider alternatives.

To reconsider any decisions that have not enhanced our retirement.

To recognize that as circumstances change, decisions may need to be remade.

To realize that the knowledge, understanding, and experiences of others can help us make sound judgments.

Group size

Groups of up to 30 participants.

Time

30 minutes.

Materials

Checklist worksheet; easel pad and markers; paper and pencils.

Process

1. Review the process of making decisions about retirement, offering some of the following comments:

   - We bring to retirement an integration of the experiences and beliefs we developed over a lifetime.

   - We base our decisions about retirement on our past experiences: our career, family, education, community, and long-term goals.

   - In retirement we have many opportunities for a change in direction. The changes we make may affect our family, participation in civic affairs, choice of living conditions, and decisions about travel and work.

   - When presented with choices, it is wise to withhold immediate judgment, taking time for careful review and consideration of alternative choices.

2. Distribute the **Checklist** worksheet to each participant and provide the following instructions:

   ➤ On the worksheet, indicate what you believe is the best choice for you by underlining the word "should" or the words "should not" in each statement.

   ➤ Because an immediate response to these questions is most likely to reflect your honest feelings, work quickly and do not go back over the statements. You will have about 5 minutes.

3. While participants are working, write the numbers 1–13 on the easel pad and head two columns with the words "should" and "should not."

4. When most people appear to have finished writing, read

aloud the thirteen items and ask people by a show of hands to indicate whether they responded to each statement with "should" or "should not." Record the numbers on the easel pad.

5. Choose the three to six items for which there are the greatest differences in response and discuss these items one at a time, asking participants why they responded as they did. Avoid giving the sense that one answer is better than another.

6. After 30 minutes, conclude the session by encouraging participants to continue gathering information about options, sharing that information with each other, and reevaluating any decisions that are not supporting a positive retirement.

Variation

- If the group is larger than thirty, you may wish to form small groups for the follow-up discussion in step 5.

  Form groups of four to six persons who disagree on a specific item. Once in the small groups, ask them to discuss their differences and prepare a short oral report. Form as many groups as there are items of major disagreement.

  Allow these small groups to meet for 10–15 minutes, then reconvene the entire group and ask a representative from each small group to report on their discussion.

Checklist*

1. I (should) (should not) spend most of my time with people my own age.

2. I (should) (should not) bow out of civic affairs and let younger people take over.

3. I (should) (should not) be greatly concerned about saving money to be left to my children.

4. I (should) (should not) spend more time with things of the spirit as I get older.

5. I (should) (should not) stop at my old place of employment to make sure things are run right.

6. By now I (should) (should not) have a will and a living will prepared.

7. I (should) (should not) rely on my children for care in my later years.

8. In choosing my retirement home it (should)) (should not) require little work to keep up.

9. I (should) (should not) expect to do additional long-term financial planning.

10. I (should) (should not) return to some hobby or special interest that I had to drop earlier.

11. I (should) (should not) consider taking on a part-time job.

12. At my age I (should) (should not) try to be a continuing learner.

13. I (should) (should not) take it as easy as I possibly can.

This is a revised version of an exercise copyrighted in 1986 by Doris and Burton Kreitlow and used extensively since that time.

12 Adapting your lifestyle to change

Using the analogy of lifestyle as a sailing ship in which we make our life journey, participants will look at the many sails which catch the wind and propel them along. They will determine how they can mend or replace these sails in case they are weakened. In short, they will discuss how they can adapt to the changes that aging brings.

Objectives

To begin making long-term plans.

To think creatively about making adaptations as needed.

To guard against inflexibility.

To confidently make good choices that maintain independence and a quality lifestyle.

Time

1 hour.

Materials

Easel pad and markers.

☞ *On the easel pad, prepare a simple drawing of a sailing ship with ten to twelve sails.*

Process

1. Introduce the topic and the goals of this exercise by making some of the following comments:

   ■ People can and should anticipate living many years in retirement.

   ■ Life expectancy for women has increased dramatically since 1900. The Census Bureau tells us that women can expect to live seventy-nine years, and men can expect to live seventy-two years. Since the average woman marries a man three years older than herself, many women eventually live alone.

   ■ Whether living with a spouse or living alone, most people consider remaining independent in their own home (whether home is a house, an apartment, a condominium, or a mobile home) to be the single most important factor in maintaining a quality lifestyle.

   ■ For people to live in their own homes, they need to obtain services such as transportation, yard and household help, and, in case of illness, personal care.

   ■ Technological advances are making it possible for people with physical handicaps to remain independent. For instance, a closet-sized modular bathroom comprising sink, shower, toilet, and tub is now on the market and can be installed in an older home that previously had its only bathroom on the second floor.

   ■ Presently 95 percent of elders are not dependent on institutional support. At any given time only about 5 percent of the elderly require nursing home care.

   ■ To maintain independence, it's essential to plan ahead and to remain flexible about change.

2. Lead participants through a short guided imagery exercise by reading aloud the following script:

Close your eyes, lean back, and picture yourself thirty years ago. Some of you will find yourself in your mid-twenties, others will see yourself in your thirties. (Pause) Where were you living? . . . Where did you work? . . . What kind of car were you driving? . . . How did you spend your day? . . . Was part of it spent caring for small children? . . . Take a moment to picture yourself at that time in your life. (Pause)

Now move ahead ten years and picture yourself again. (Pause) Were you still living in the same place? . . . Were you in the same job? . . . What kind of a car did you have? . . . Did you have more free time to develop a hobby?

Now let's advance ten more years. Take a moment to picture yourself as you were then. (Pause) Are you in the same house? Or have you moved? . . . Do you have the same job and the same responsibilities? . . . Are your children still in school or have they left your home?

Now let the past go, open your eyes, and rejoin the present realizing how flexible you have been in adjusting to all the changes that have happened during the past thirty years. In ten, twenty, or thirty years of retirement you can expect similar changes. As you anticipate and plan for those changes, don't forget how adept you have become at dealing with change after years of practice.

3. Select participants who have been retired for ten years or so to act as experts for this step of the exercise. Ask the experts the following questions:

    ✔ What type of lifestyle changes have you made since you have retired?

    ✔ How did you implement these changes?

    ✔ Did you use any advance planning for these changes?

4. Allow participants 5–10 minutes to discuss changes such as moving, death of a spouse, health problems, diminished energy for some hard physical tasks, changes in sport activities, and dissatisfaction with their home neighborhood.

☞ *If the group is composed of preretirees, ask about the changes their parents have made as they attained their late seventies and eighties.*

5. Turn to the sailing ship drawing on the easel pad and present the metaphor of life as a ship.

6. Explain to participants that the sails which propel a ship and keep it on course will be compared to the essential elements that keep our ship of life moving and give us a fine steady course. Write on one of the sails: "a comfortable, well-planned home." As the group names other essentials for a satisfying retirement, write them on the sails. If the following items are not mentioned, place each of them on a sail:

- Health, our own and our partner's
- Mobility (the ability to walk and to drive a car)
- Availability of essential services (medical, dental, library, postal, banking, transportation, household and yard help)
- Good companions
- Financial security
- Safety and serenity
- Energy and interest to accomplish tasks

7. After the participants have developed a list similar to this, number the sails and form a small group for each by asking participants to count off. Each small group will discuss the topic on the specified sail. Allow any who wish to join a specific group for personal reasons to do so. Give the following instructions:

➤ Appoint a secretary to record interesting and creative ideas to share with the whole group and choose a spokesperson to make your group's presentation.

➤ Through discussion, determine how your group's "sail"

can be strengthened or replaced if changing circumstances make this necessary. If, for example, illness threatens your ability to remain in your comfortable home, consider options and adaptations that would make it possible to maintain an independent life. You will have 15 minutes for this process.

☞ *Circulate among the groups as they brainstorm. If they have difficulty generating ideas, be prepared to offer suggestions about community resources.*

8. Reconvene the entire group and discuss planning in advance for change, starting at the beginning of the list with "Comfortable, well-planned home" and proceeding through to the last item.

9. In closing, summarize the session with the following statement:

   ■ What people fear most about aging is being unable to care for themselves because of disability. Although at times we may have to use nursing home care for recuperation, it is a fact that only 5 percent of elders actually live in nursing homes. Advance planning, creative alternatives, and the willingness to adapt to change will help people maintain independence and a quality lifestyle indefinitely. Sometimes this means paid help in one's own home. If so, it is the best bargain around.

13 Housing and possessions

Some people love to collect things; others discard what they don't use; and still others will throw away almost anything. In this exercise, participants explore their relationship to possessions and the effect that has on retirement decisions.

Objectives

To develop a clearer idea of our own external and internal valuing of home and possessions.

To understand how the way in which we value our possessions affects the decisions we make.

To become more objective in evaluating our changes in our energy, our physical competency, and the expectations others have of us.

Group size

Unlimited.

Time

60–90 minutes.

Materials

Possessions scale worksheets; pencils.

Process

1. Introduce this exercise to participants by making some of the following comments about the value people place on their homes and their possessions.

   ■ What is it that people in our culture prize most? Most often it's their home. The major financial asset of most older Americans is their home. Over the years people devote time and money to expanding, remodeling, landscaping, decorating, and caring for their homes, but beyond the dollar value of housing, the place called home provides comfort and security.

- To move from a large family home to a smaller one or to an apartment, condominium, group home, or care facility is one of the most difficult and stressful decisions older persons may ever make.

- People also prize other possessions, those with financial value, such as a car, truck, boat, mobile home, or all terrain vehicle, and those with emotional value, such as two thousand slides and snapshots of children, books, old school notes, love letters, and mementos of vacations.

- These possessions are more than physical objects. They represent the memories of good feelings we have in their presence, the comfort we find in their nearness, the security represented by their value. Feelings about possessions often are more important than their material value.

- If you allow yourself to be in physical or emotional bondage to the things you own, your possessions can be a burden rather than a blessing.

2. Tell participants that you are going to read a letter that was received by the authors of this book from one of their cousins. Cousin Lorraine said she would be happy to have them share her letter. Ask them to listen carefully to the role that home and possessions played in Lorraine's situation. (The letter is printed on pages 76 and 77.)

☞ *In response to my request to use her letter, including the names, in workshops, Lorraine wrote, "Sure you can use our names and the letter. If it helps convince one couple to move sooner than we did, it'll be worthwhile."*

---

3. After reading the letter, lead a discussion based on the questions below.

☞ *Suggest to participants who are retired and in their sixties, seventies, eighties, or beyond to consider all questions in terms of themselves. Younger participants can do likewise, or they may want to respond in terms of their parents' experience.*

✔ Why does decision-making on housing take so long?

✔ What should be the role of grown children in dealing with parents who remain attached to the family home long after it would be wiser to move?

✔ What elements lead to added stress if a couple or individual fails to make a move in time?

✔ How can we prepare ourselves for decisions so they do not come as a surprise?

✔ What positive elements do you see in Lorraine's letter?

4. Begin the second part of this exercise by making the following comments:

■ When it was necessary for Lorraine to move, she had to make a multitude of decisions about her possessions.

■ For some people, decisions about which items to keep and which to discard are easy to make, for others they are very difficult.

■ You will now have a chance to think about the value you place on things that you own.

5. Distribute the **Possession scale** worksheet to each participant and provide the following instructions:

➤ Read and answer all four questions. There are no right or wrong answers, and you will not be asked to share your score with others.

➤ Count the X's for each question and record that number on the line provided.

➤ Using the chart at the end of the worksheet, compute your final score.

➤ You do not need to share your score with others in the group.

6. Following the completion of the **Possession scale** worksheet, ask participants to total their scores and encourage them to discuss the following questions without identifying their own scores.

✔ What are the advantages and disadvantages of being:

an externally oriented person?

an internally oriented person?

a person with a balance between internal and external orientation?

✔ Does increasing age influence the manner in which people view their home and possessions? In what ways?

✔ If you anticipate that your attachment to your possessions may bring problems in the future, what steps could you take right now to avoid those problems?

7. Conclude by asking participants to share any additional insights they gained during the activity.

Variations

■ If time is limited, steps 1–3 can be completed in one session and steps 4–6 in another. In either case, conclude with step 7.

■ If you are working with a large number of people, form small groups to discuss the questions in step 3, assigning them each one question. After 10 minutes, reconvene to listen to reports from a representative of each group.

©1997 Whole Person Press 210 W Michigan Duluth MN 55802   (800) 247-6789

January 1995

Dear Burt and Doris,

It's about time I wrote you a long letter after getting three from you. That didn't mean I didn't appreciate them. They were much appreciated since I was so busy taking care of John, the house, the yard and all our finances! You see John has been on the way down for five years, noticeable to me. The last two were the worst.

Besides all his physical problems, he had senile dementia, almost complete current memory loss, so it was very hard for him (and me).

He broke his hip September 21, 1994, and had his hip replaced the 22nd. He was hospitalized five days and then moved to the nursing home across the street from my apartment.

God had a hand in that. We had been looking at many apartments, and John turned them all down. He really did not want to leave our house, but the kids convinced him he was being selfish as it was getting too difficult for me to do it all.

John and I again went looking for an apartment and when he saw this one he said, "that's more like it," and we rented it that day, Friday, September 9th. We paid the October rent.

We sold our house August 7th. The closing was to be on October 14. Meanwhile I was packing alone, since John wasn't physically able to even care for himself then.

Son Ed, in Arizona, heard of my moving plans and said he was coming to help spruce up the place for sale and would stay as long as it took. He came July 5th and hauled away three truckloads of junk to various recycling places. He stayed a week. I surely was grateful.

When we were getting ready to move John fell in between all of the boxes on the carpeted living room floor! I called 911 for the fifth time, and he never did come back to live in the house or to the apartment.

I had an estate sale's person sell all our extra stuff and they wanted us out October 3 before the sale, which was sched-

©1997 Whole Person Press 210 W Michigan Duluth MN 55802   (800) 247-6789

uled on October 7th and 8th. Well, John was in the nursing home during the move. Gladys and daughter Nancy helped me move October 3rd. They were just great.

Meanwhile, we had to get a lawyer to give Jeanette power of attorney for John so we could sign the ten papers at the closing on the house October 12th. We had to have our realtor, lawyer, social service worker, daughter, myself, and John present. We had to choose a day when John was cognizant enough to give his permission. That was not easy—getting six busy people in one place at one time!

These were the most stressful days of my life. Although I was eating well, I lost twenty pounds in ten days. I was glad I had it to lose.

I still haven't got my finances straightened out. I have a financial advisor and lawyer working on it.

Friday, Saturday, and Sunday of Christmas weekend I had a viral infection and 102 temperature and spent it all in bed. (I didn't even care.) Now I am finally over it and feel fine.

I love my apartment, the building, and the people here, who have been just wonderful to me. One lady was from my old neighborhood and came to my ceramic classes; so she got me into their group of six friends, and we do things together.

We had a blizzard the day of John's reviewal but forty-nine braved the weather. One hundred and fifty people came to the funeral. One hundred came for lunch. I got two hundred sympathy cards. Everyone was so thoughtful. I even heard from my Normal Training classmates! It surely helped ease the hurt.

Son Ed flew in for the funeral. Sharon and Steve drove in from Virginia. Nancy's family and Jeanette and Greg from Chaska were all here, of course.

Keep traveling and having fun while you still can. And thanks for all those letters you've sent.

Lovingly,

Cousin Lorraine

Possession scale

1. Place an X after each of the items you
   tend to save for five or more years:

   Family slides, snapshots, and negatives   _____
   Memorabilia from vacations   _____
   Physical items tied to past work   _____
   All the issues of at least one magazine   _____

   #1 Score   _____

2. Place an X after the items you have
   systematically replaced over the years?

   Kitchen equipment   _____
   Furniture   _____
   TV's, radios, CD's, phones   _____
   Wall hangings, framed paintings   _____

   #2 Score   _____

3. Place an X after the items that are
   very dear to your heart?

   My home   _____
   My cars   _____
   My family heirlooms   _____
   My collections (stamps, paintings, rocks)   _____
   My books   _____
   My condo or vacation home   _____

   #3 Score   _____

4. If you had to move to a home with one-half
   of your present living space, which three of
   the following six items would you give up
   first? Mark those items with an X.

   My collection of family memorabilia   _____
   Materials for my hobbies   _____
   Old books, magazines, clippings   _____

Things stored to use later　＿＿＿＿
Old chairs, tables, household equipment　＿＿＿＿
Anything that takes up too much space　＿＿＿＿

#4 Score　＿＿＿＿

Use this chart to determine your score for each question.

For item 1:
If no X, enter 0
If 1 or 2, enter 1
If 3 or 4, enter 2

For item 2:
If no X, enter 0
If 1 or 2, enter 1
If 3 or 4, enter 2

For item 3:
If 5 or 6, enter 0
If 3 or 4, enter 1
If 1 or 2, enter 2
If no X, enter 3

For item 4:
If 2 or 3 from the first three, enter 2
If 2 or 3 from the last three, enter 0
All other combinations, enter 1

Add your scores to obtain total score. Total score = ＿＿＿

If your total score is:

7, 8, or 9	You tend to be externally oriented, valuing the possessions you worked to obtain for your family
3, 4, 5, or 6	You are balanced in orientation.
0, 1, or 2	You tend to be internally oriented, valuing memories of home and family.

©1997 Whole Person Press 210 W Michigan Duluth MN 55802　(800) 247-6789

14 A new lifestyle

When employment no longer mandates where we live or how we spend our time, we are free to choose from a variety of exciting lifestyle options. This exercise focuses on some of those choices.

Objectives

To recognize that lifestyle is a composite of where, how, and with whom we live and how we focus our time and energy.

To become aware that there are pluses and minuses related to all choices about lifestyle.

To realize that when initial choices about lifestyle are found to be inadequate, they can be changed.

Group size

Up to 40.

Time

60 minutes.

Materials

Lifestyle choices worksheet; easel pad and markers; paper and pencils.

☞ *Prior to meeting with the group, prepare four signs, labeling them in large print "Stay in home," "Move to new home," "Maintain two homes," and "Mobile lifestyle," and place one sign in each corner of the room.*

Process

1. Introduce the exercise to participants with an enthusi-

astic statement about the exciting lifestyle options open to retirees. Continue by explaining that our lifestyle results from crucial choices that are best made prior to or early in retirement. These lifestyle choices must allow for change. The crucial choices are:

- **Geographic location.** For the first time since we were young adults, home can truly be where our heart is. We can live where we want to. We can stay, or we can move.

- **Housing.** We could refurbish our family home for retirement or build or buy. We might have two homes, using our vacation home for longer periods of the year than ever before.

- **Companions.** We can choose where and with whom we want to spend our time, but we do need to consider our spouse's wishes and think about family and friends we may wish to be near.

- **Central focus.** We can choose between productive work and leisure opportunities. Or we can decide to combine both.

- **Specific interests or needs.** The desire to follow a personal interest or the need to address health concerns can influence our decisions.

- **Income.** Our income and assets will determine what we can afford, but even those of us with lower incomes should examine each of the six considerations.

2. Distribute the **Lifestyle choices** worksheet to participants and ask them, as they hear descriptions of two very different lifestyles, to consider the choices these couples have made. Read **Example 1** and **Example 2** on pages 83 and 84.

3. Ask participants to do for themselves what the couples in the examples have done—make crucial choices about their own retirement lifestyle. Provide the following

instructions for completion of the worksheet and allow 5 minutes for the process.

➤ Those of you who have not yet retired should assume that you have complete freedom to do whatever you believe would be deeply fulfilling. Your only restriction is your anticipated income.

➤ Those of you who have already begun retirement should assess your satisfaction with the choices you have made and list any changes you would like to make.

4. Form small groups based on the choice of where to live, giving the following instructions:

➤ Each corner of the room is labeled with a different type of living option. Select the one that you prefer and go to that corner of the room.

➤ Choose one member of your group to be the spokesperson and another to be the secretary. The spokesperson is to lead a discussion of the questions on the easel pad while the secretary jots down answers and comments to the questions.

➤ You will have 15 minutes for this process.

☞ *Prior to the session, print the discussion questions below on the easel pad.*

✔ What specific considerations made you make this choice?

✔ Can you foresee any difficulties you might have to overcome?

✔ What is the greatest "plus" for you from this choice?

✔ What is the greatest "minus" for you from this choice?

✔ In case you decide this choice is not satisfactory, what options do you have for changing or rectifying it?

✔ After twenty years of retirement, you may need to

make changes in the lifestyle you have chosen. Can this choice be easily adapted, or would it be necessary for you then to select a totally new lifestyle?

5. Reconvene the entire group and ask the spokesperson for each group to give a brief report on the responses from their group.

☞ *In case one corner draws no participants, the leader should summarize the pluses or minuses of that choice and then elicit comments from the group.*

6. In conclusion, briefly review the items on the **Lifestyle choices** worksheet. For each item, ask one participant to respond with the most significant insight they heard expressed.

Variation

▪ Instead of forming small groups for step 4, hold up the four signs, one at a time, for discussion. Ask those who would choose this option to answer the questions. This variation could be used if the group exceeds forty participants.

Example 1

Jane and John have an exotic lifestyle. This is a second marriage for each after the loss of a spouse. Both brought good retirement incomes to their second marriage since both were retired professors. Both Jane and John have married children and grandchildren. The place they elected to live is Oahu, Hawaii, where they have now made their home for fifteen years. Their home is a rented bungalow, part of a retirement complex. In addition to bungalows, the complex includes a high-rise apartment building and a nursing home. The decision to live here was part of this couple's long-term plan. It gives them additional options if health problems develop. They chose to limit their contact with children and

©1997 Whole Person Press 210 W Michigan Duluth MN 55802   (800) 247-6789

grandchildren to annual visits. Contacts with old friends also were reduced, but they have established new friendships, particularly through their focus interest. Jane and John both wanted to continue to work in their professional fields of botany and entomology, so before arranging anything else, they offered their services without pay to the Bishop Museum in Honolulu. They work there as volunteers from four to six hours every weekday. They do not have a car, instead use bus and taxi transportation. One factor in their choice of Hawaii for retirement was Jane's need for a warm climate. Their goals for personal development include travel and study that will enable them to grow in expertise. They take one long trip each year to places like China, New Guinea, and Africa. Their lifestyle is expensive, but they can afford it, and they enjoy it.

Example 2

When Harry retired from his job as a county assessor, he and his wife, Doris, decided they had no desire to leave their home community where their children and grandchildren also live. For years they had enjoyed a cabin on a beautiful lake ten miles from town. Now they move out there in spring and stay for much of the year. Several years after retirement, they sold the family home and bought a condominium in the downtown area because Harry's health problems made him eager to eliminate some yard and house maintenance. Now, twenty years into retirement, they maintain both their cabin and their condominium with some housekeeping assistance. They thoroughly enjoy the change of scene that the two homes give them. Their focus is mainly family, church, and leisure activities. Their health needs can be met locally, and they limit their travel to short trips by car. They live well within their retirement income.

Lifestyle choices
Place or location
Housing
Significant companions
Focus interest
Special interest or need
Income considerations

15 Our community is "us"

Participants will explore options for community involvement and will consider their own level of comfort with
participation and with taking leadership roles.

Objectives

To understand that community involvement is an opportunity as well as a responsibility.

To realize that age is not a discriminating factor for volunteers working to improve their communities.

To identify how comfortable we are with community
participation.

Group size

10–50 is optimum.

Time

60 minutes.

Materials

Community involvement worksheets; pencils; easel pad
and markers.

Process

1. Introduce the benefits of community involvement by
   making the following comments:

   ■ Interviews with 140 elders chosen as the most positive retirees in their communities demonstrated that,
   almost without exception, they were involved in community service.

   ■ Another research study investigated retirees making new lives for themselves in Florida and Sun City,

Arizona. The people studied were risk-takers who found productive tasks as they fit into their new communities. The researchers concluded that, in comparison to more passive retirees, these adventurous elders had higher self-esteem and better physical and mental health.

2. Read aloud the story below, introducing it by saying it illustrates what a few committed people can do.

John was a small Wisconsin town's most eligible bachelor until he married Hazel, a nurse from nearby Madison. The couple bought a home, and Hazel soon became an active participant in the life of their small community. However, summer temperatures often soar in mid-Wisconsin, and Hazel, who loved to swim, missed the opportunity to get to a beach.

One steaming July day as Hazel put lunch on the table, she mopped her perspiring face and said to John, "Why don't they build a swimming pool in this town?"

John grinned and said, "Hazel, honey, when are you going to realize that THEY is US?"

Seven years later, the town did have a swimming pool.

The initial $100,000 came from a bequest made by the last member of one of the town's founding families. But the project also took lots of effort on the part of John, Hazel, and other citizens.

3. After reading the story, share the following comment with participants:

■ The communities we live in provide us with close human relationships and opportunities to share the responsibilities of everyday life with others. These communities range in size from neighborhoods to small towns to whole counties. In them, we share a geographic location, business and government services of all kinds, and a common interest in making the place we live a very good place.

4. Ask participants to respond with a show of hands if they agree with the statements that follow. Encourage brief discussion of each statement, but limit the total discussion time to 5 minutes.

- I believe that equal rights for every citizen also means equal responsibility for every citizen.

- If I vote and pay my taxes, I'm off the hook as far as community responsibility goes.

- I believe that once you reach retirement age you should hand over civic jobs to the younger generation.

5. Distribute the **Community involvement** worksheets and introduce the activity with the following comments:

- Some people like to work in groups; others prefer to work alone. Some people enjoy making fiery speeches; others would rather work behind the scenes. No matter what your preference is, you can be a positive force in your community.

- If you prefer the support of a group, organizations such as Lions, Rotary, women's clubs, garden clubs, and many others give you the opportunity to work with friends on worthwhile projects.

- If you prefer to initiate action on your own, you'll need knowledge, commitment, and the willingness to take risks.

- Your preferences about how and when to act will be indicated by the choices you make on this worksheet. If your score indicates that you are uncomfortable taking a visible, active role in your community, you may need to look for other ways to fulfill your citizenship tasks. You will have 10 minutes to complete the worksheet.

- Place a check beside the response which most closely represents your reaction to the situation.

6. While participants are working, copy the answer key that follows on the easel pad.

Situation	a	b	c	d
#1	2	1	3	4
#2	1	2	3	4
#3	1	2	3	4
#4	4	1	3	2
#5	3	4	2	1
#6	3	4	1	2
#7	2	3	1	4
#8	1	2	3	4

7. When participants have completed the worksheet, direct their attention to the answer key and give the following instructions:

➤ Use the key on the easel to find the score for each answer, then record it in the appropriate space in the worksheet's scoring section.

➤ Add the scores to get your total. For each question, a score of 1 indicates a lack of interest or a low comfort level. A score of 4 suggests that you enjoy that form of community involvement.

A total score of 8–13 suggests that you are interested in learning about your community's needs, but you may not feel ready for active involvement. If your score is 14–19, you may be willing to help but you may not know how to get started. Perhaps you don't recognize the value of your skills. A score of 21–26 suggests that you are a willing worker who sometimes takes a leadership role. If your score is 27–32, it's likely that you are already a community activist.

➤ If you would like to become involved in your community but tend to be uncomfortable with group activity or are reluctant to take a leadership role, review your worksheet to discover areas in which your score suggests a higher level of comfort. Those might be good places for you to start. Take a few minutes and record any new insights about how you might become more involved in your community.

8. Summarize the session by making the following comments, adding your own insights.

■ If you feel a commitment to help address a need, don't let lack of knowledge stop you; no one ever starts a community project with all the answers.

■ A bonus of working for the community is the excitement of learning new things. It's a stimulating process.

■ Seek information about community needs from the newspaper, organizations, friends, and policy makers.

■ Your ideas are worthwhile; you have valuable experience; and your suggestions can make a difference.

■ Official backing from policy makers is vital. If you are going to be a committee, be an official committee.

■ The wider you can spread knowledge of what you are doing, the more support you will gain. Don't be afraid to publish and speak about your views.

■ The people with whom you work closely to accomplish something good for the community will very likely become your friends.

Variations

■ After step 8, form groups of four to six persons. Assign one or two of the situations on the worksheet to each group and ask them to work out a way that a citizen's committee could accomplish the task.

■ The summary at the session's end might include a chance for individuals to express their own comfort level in dealing with community involvement.

Community involvement

1. The community hospital needs extensive modernization. The local newspaper has outlined the need.
   a. John commented at the coffee shop, "I suppose this means the taxpayers will be hit again, but I'll support it."
   b. Mary read the paper but ignored the problem.
   c. Ted stopped at the hospital administrator's office and asked what he could do to help.
   d. Nancy called the mayor and volunteered to help form or join a task force to study the problem.

2. The town library is about to burst at the seams. A new library building is essential.
   a. Thelma sees the chaos every time she goes to the library and ignores it.
   b. James and his wife discussed the problem when the preschool story hour was dropped for lack of space.
   c. Bob talked about the need to the librarian.
   d. Lucille and Mary helped form a Library Friends group to gain support for a new building.

3. The senior center has little to offer but cards and meals. Attendance is down, and financial support is threatened.
   a. Roger complained to his cribbage partner about the other seniors who never show up.
   b. Mabel suggested that a bake sale might spark interest.
   c. Bill asked the coordinator what he could do to help.
   d. Mildred formed a committee to find some interesting programs and events.

4. The county board asked for ideas on starting a recycling program.
   a. Sally and Dianna decided this was their cause. They volunteered to head a county recycling committee.
   b. Steve commented at a chamber of commerce meeting that "recycling is a waste of time for businesses."
   c. Joanne asked her garden club for ideas to pass on to the county board.
   d. Gilbert told his wife, "If someone starts recycling we'll go along, but I don't know how they'd go about it."

5. The public health department is attempting to organize a low cost annual cancer clinic. Volunteers are needed.
    a. George called and asked to volunteer.
    b. Marlene, a retired nurse, called to offer her help.
    c. Tom commented to his wife that they should both get a checkup through this clinic.
    d. Donna said, " I'll go next year if they have it again."

6. A committee was established to help the city develop a youth center. Senior citizens were urged to volunteer.
    a. Charlotte suggested that the committee hold their planning meetings in the senior center.
    b. Keith volunteered to ask the Golden Age Club for help.
    c. Vi said when she was young kids made their own fun, but she'd be willing to bake cookies.
    d. Steve said he would help if he was needed.

7. The Lutheran church needs help to present an annual community Christmas concert using local talent.
    a. Betty was not a musician, but she called and volunteered to help with publicity and typing the program.
    b. Hilda and her husband from the Baptist Church volunteered to recruit singers from their choir.
    c. John, a good tenor, told his wife he was too busy to practice, but they should attend the event.
    d. Marjorie volunteered to find a director and organist.

8. Dale told fellow Rotarians that instruction for women in financial planning was badly needed in the community.
    a. Bret said, "Turn the idea over to adult community education."
    b. Herb said "AARP has good teaching materials for this. I'll give you the address."
    c. Steve, the town banker, said, "We'd be glad to provide meeting space and act as sponsor for the class."
    d. Dave, an insurance provider said, "Dale, if you, Herb, and Steve will help, I'm willing to teach the class."

Scoring: 1.____   2.____   3.____   4.____

5.____   6.____   7.____   8.____ **TOTAL** ____

©1997 Whole Person Press 210 W Michigan Duluth MN 55802   (800) 247-6789

A rich life in retirement

16 Financial risk: how much can you handle?

In this exercise, participants assess the level of financial risk with which they are comfortable. They relate this comfort level to the financial investments they have already made and the potential growth for those investments. Alternatives can then be examined.

Objectives

To determine a personal risk-comfort level so that financial investment decisions can be made with a sound balance between financial gain and peace of mind.

To develop a strategy for investments.

Group size

10–20.

Time

30–40 minutes.

Materials

Easel pad and markers; **How much risk can you handle?** worksheets and pencils.

☞ *Some people are reluctant to discuss personal financial matters. Allow them to participate in the discussion without asking them to contribute more than they are comfortable sharing.*

Process

1. Introduce the exercise with the following comments about investments:

- Everyone planning for retirement and investing for the future must determine the amount of risk with which they are comfortable. Some of us are by nature very conservative, others are aggressive.

- Aggressive, risky investments and conservative, safe investments tend to grow at different rates.

  Using Rule 72, you can calculate how long it will take your money to double if it is earning compound interest. Simply divide 72 by the interest rate on your investment. If, for instance, an investment returns 7 percent interest, your money will double in 10 years. An investment earning 14 percent will double in five years, but the accompanying risk is likely to be much greater.

- Investment decisions are necessary for those who are determined to save for retirement or for their heirs.

- Your responses to questions on the worksheet you complete today will suggest where you stand on a four-level scale from conservative to aggressive. The conservative investments tend to show less growth, and you may be discontent with that growth.

- On the other hand, the aggressive investor may enjoy higher rewards but have trouble sleeping at night.

- Knowing where you stand can be a springboard for serious thinking about your total investment strategy.

2. Distribute the worksheets and allow time for participants to read and respond to each of the ten items.

3. While people are completing the worksheet, copy the following chart on the easel pad. When everyone is finished, ask them to score their worksheet by referring to the chart and then to total their scores on a separate sheet of paper.

©1997 Whole Person Press 210 W Michigan Duluth MN 55802   (800) 247-6789

Situation	a	b	c	d
#1	4	1	3	2
#2	1	4	2	3
#3	3	4	2	1
#4	2	3	1	4
#5	3	4	2	1
#6	4	3	2	1
#7	1	3	2	4
#8	2	3	4	1
#9	4	3	2	1
#10	2	3	1	4

4. After the scores are totalled, help participants interpret their meaning by reading the following analysis:

10–17   You're a conservative investor. You don't like to take chances with your money. You won't reap big profits, but you'll feel safe.

18–25   You're a semiconservative investor, a person who sticks with safe investing most of the time but who will take a small chance when given enough information.

26–32   You're a semiaggressive investor. You're willing to take chances with your money if you think the odds of high earnings are in your favor.

33–40   You're an aggressive investor. You look for every opportunity to make your money grow, even though the odds may be long. You think of money as a tool for making more money; you don't tuck it away to grow slowly and safely.

5. If it appears that participants would be comfortable discussing financial matters, ask them to share any insights they gained from completing the worksheet and any changes in investment strategy they might want to consider in light of their answers.

©1997 Whole Person Press 210 W Michigan Duluth MN 55802   (800) 247-6789

6. In closing, make the following comments to the group:

- Your score need not be shared in this group, but it would be wise for couples or even an entire family to discuss the results.

- Likewise if you work with a retirement or financial planner, it would be well to share the results with that person.

Variations

- If participants are accustomed to working together and are open to sharing personal financial information, this exercise can be done in groups of four to six people. After completing the worksheet and discussing their answers, each small group should be asked to share with the total group the items on which they all agree and the items on which they have major disagreement. These items can then be discussed.

- For those with great interest in financial planning, an ongoing study group may be formed. The book *Feathering Your Nest, The Retirement Planner* makes a good text for this type of group.

"How Much Risk Can You Handle?" from *Feathering Your Nest, The Retirement Planner* by Lisa Berger. Reprinted by permission of Workman Publishing Company, Inc. All rights reserved.

How much risk can you handle?

Place an (X) in the left margin before the response which most nearly reflects how you would react.

1. Two weeks after buying 100 shares of $20 stock, the price leaps up to over $30. You decide to:

   a. Buy more stock—it's obviously a winner.

   b. Sell your stock and take your profits.

   c. Sell half your stock to recoup some cost and hold on to the remainder.

   d. Do nothing and wait for it to advance further.

2. You win $300 in an office football pool. You:

   a. Spend it on groceries.

   b. Try to boost your good fortune further and purchase lottery tickets.

   c. Put it in a money market fund.

   d. Put it in your brokerage account to buy stock.

3. On days when the stock market takes big jumps, you:

   a. Wish you owned more stock but do nothing.

   b. Call your broker and ask for recommendations.

   c. Feel glad you're not in the market, being whipsawed by its gyrations.

   d. Pay little attention to how it moves.

4. You're planning a Caribbean vacation and can either lock in a fixed room-and-meal rate of $150 per day or book standby and pay anywhere from $100 to $300 per day. You:

   a. Grab the fixed-rate deal.

   b. Talk to friends who have been there about availability of last-minute accommodations.

   c. Book standby and also arrange vacation insurance because you're leery of the tour operator.

   d. Take your chances with standby.

©1997 Whole Person Press 210 W Michigan Duluth MN 55802   (800) 247-6789

5. The owner of your apartment building is converting units to condos. Tenants like you can buy their apartments for $75,000 or sell their option for $12,000.

On the open market, units have recently sold for close to $100,000 and their price seems to be going up. For financing, you'll have to borrow the down payment and carry mortgage and condo fees higher than your present rent. You:

a. Buy your apartment.

b. Buy your apartment and look around to buy another.

c. Sell the option and arrange to rent the apartment yourself.

d. Sell the option and move out because you think the conversion will attract couples with small children.

6. You have been working for three years for a privately owned management consulting firm that has been growing strongly. As a senior executive, you are offered the option of purchasing up to 2 percent of company stock—2,000 shares at $10 a share. Although the company is privately owned, its majority owner has successfully, and lucratively, sold three other businesses, and intends to sell this one eventually. You decide to:

a. Purchase all the shares you can and tell the owner you would invest more if allowed to do so.

b. Purchase all the shares.

c. Purchase half the shares.

d. Purchase only a token number of shares.

7. You go to Atlantic City for the first time, walk through the gambling hall, then pick a game. You choose:

a. Quarter slot machines.

b. $5 minimum-bet roulette.

c. Dollar slot machines.

d. $25 minimum-bet blackjack.

8. For a friend's birthday, you want to take him to a special memorable restaurant. However, your friend lives in a city you don't know, so to find this restaurant, you:

   a. Read restaurant reviews in the local newspapers.

   b. Ask coworkers if they know of a suitable restaurant.

   c. Call the only other person you know in this distant city, someone who eats out a lot but only recently moved there.

   d. Visit the city one evening before your special dinner to check out restaurants and their menus.

9. The expression that best describes your lifestyle is:

   a. No guts, no glory.

   b. Just do it!

   c. Look before you leap.

   d. All good things come to those who wait.

10. Your attitude toward money is best described as:

   a. A dollar saved is a dollar earned.

   b. You've got to spend money to make money.

   c. Cash and carry only.

   d. Wherever possible, use other people's money.

©1997 Whole Person Press 210 W Michigan Duluth MN 55802 (800) 247-6789

17 To our good health

By interviewing a medical professional and meeting in small groups formed around health concerns, participants will consider their responsibility for preserving their own health.

Objectives

To accept responsibility for guardianship of our own health.

To discover sources of information about personal health problems.

To learn to communicate openly with our physicians, to ask questions, and to participate in decisions.

Group size

Unlimited.

Time

1 –½ hours.

Materials

Health concern signs for locating small group meetings— Heart, Vision, Diabetes, Gastrointestinal, Allergies and Asthma, Hearing, Cancer, Blood Pressure and Stroke, Bone Problems, Other (this group may need to be divided); paper and pencils.

☞ *Prior to the session, tape the health concern signs on the walls, leaving space for groups to gather near each sign.*

Process

1. Begin the session by making the following comments about the value of taking personal responsibility for one's own health.

- Health and mobility are the greatest treasures we possess, yet when we have a health problem, many of us have to be coerced into seeing a doctor. A fact we must face is that we alone are responsible for guarding and preserving our health and mobility.Our families will rest more easily if they know we are assuming this responsibility. So how do we take charge?

    First, by recognizing our own personal vulnerabilities (whether they come from genetics, a lifetime of poor health habits, or a poorly functioning immune system).

    Second, by learning all we can about the health problems we have.

    Third, by seeking out doctors with whom we have mutual liking, trust, and open communication, and then by following their advice.

    Fourth, by adopting a positive mental attitude, expecting the best, not the worst, and by looking forward to attaining our goals.

2. After the introduction, explain to participants that the first part of the session will be conducted as a 30–minute question and answer interview with a health authority. This can be done in one of two different ways.

    - You can arrange for a "live" interview with a physician or a public health professional who works with older adults. Look for someone who communicates well. Begin by asking some of the questions that begin on page 105. Participants will ask additional questions, but insure that a variety of topics are discussed.

    - If it is not possible to obtain the services of a health care professional, encourage participants to take turns reading and answering the questions, one asking the questions, another playing the role of the doctor and answering them.

3. After 30 minutes, call time on the interview portion of this exercise and summarize by stating that, although we age at different rates and in different ways, we all experience some feelings of vulnerability as we grow older.

4. Give the following instructions for formation of small groups:

➤ We will now form interest groups where you can share questions and information about specific health concerns. Note the eleven signs posted around the room and go to the discussion group of most interest to you.

➤ Select a group leader along with a reporter, who will record the group's questions and concerns and who will also act as timekeeper.

5. After the groups have assembled and selected a leader and reporter, distribute paper and pencils, then read aloud the following instructions, which you should previously have printed on the easel pad.

➤ Introduce yourself to your group, then very briefly state your personal health concern. (2 minutes each)

➤ Write a clear statement of a health concern you would like to discuss with your doctor. Specify the signs and symptoms you have. If you have pain, explain the frequency of it, the time of day you notice it, and, on a scale of 1–10, the degree of pain you experience from it. Then, on the basis of your statement, compose one direct question to ask your doctor. (5 minutes)

➤ If you are willing, share your question with others in your group.

6. At the end of 30 minutes, reconvene the entire group and ask each reporter to identify one or two concerns and questions which came up in their group.

☞ *If participants believe they need a second session on taking charge of their health, plan for it at this time.*

7. Conclude the session by summarizing the following points:

- We often go to the doctor and do not get the help or information we need. To avoid having this happen, we need to assume responsibility for insisting on clear communication and a helpful course of action.

- We must make our concerns clear even if we need to write them out in advance to do so.

- We must ask questions and pursue answers so that good two-way communication is established.

Variations

- If a second session is requested, suggest that participants do personal research in advance using the paperback book *Aging in Good Health* or other reliable publications.

- If the group is larger than 50, subdivide the interest groups so that not more than eight persons take part in each. When groups report, limit time allowed to one case from each group.

- In groups that are smaller than 20, the leader may combine several of the small groups, for example, vision and hearing or heart and blood pressure. Each group should have at least two members.

The questions in the **Interview with a Health Authority** *were developed from material in* Aging in Good Health *by Mark H. Beers, M.D. and Stephen K. Urice, Ph.D., J.D. (Pocket Books, a division of Simon & Schuster Inc. New York, N.Y. Copyright 1992. $10.00.)*

©1997 Whole Person Press 210 W Michigan Duluth MN 55802   (800) 247-6789

Interview with a health authority

Question: My doctor does not seem to have sympathy for or even any understanding of older persons. I get discouraged, and I wonder if you would advise changing doctors?

■ Geriatricians are doctors who specialize in geriatric medicine and the unique changes and diseases of older adults. While good internists or family doctors can take care of older people, there are times when it is important to have the expertise of a geriatrician—specifically, when there are sudden changes in physical or mental condition, when hospitalization or surgery is required, or in cases where complications occur from medication.

■ A good personal physician is a confidant to whom we can talk about our most intimate health problems. It is important also that we do not accept the stock answer, "At your age you have to expect parts to wear out." If you receive that response, tell your doctor you want facts so you can understand what is happening. If you can't get information that satisfies you, try another doctor.

Question: I don't feel any older than when I was fifty, but I will be sixty-eight on my next birthday. When am I going to feel my age?

■ Gerontologists differentiate between chronological age and biological age. Some people are old biologically in their fifties; others remain young into their eighties. Psychological aging is measured by how actively involved we are in working toward goals, taking responsibility, and being productive and creative. As we grow older we represent individual combinations of these three processes. Unlike Jack Benny, we cannot chronologically be thirty-nine forever, but fortunate are those who age slowly or seemingly not at all biologically and psychologically.

Question: I feel fine, but my wife says my hearing is not good. Also by seven in the evening, I notice I have "had it for the day." I'm ready to sit down and put my feet up. It's evident to me that we hardly notice these changes in ourselves at first. Is that true?

- The inside story is that virtually all of our cells change as we age. Cells become less active, stop multiplying, and in general slow down. Cell changes bring about hormonal changes. White blood cells produce fewer antibodies. Organic changes in the liver and kidneys make us react more acutely to medications. If we recognize that we tire more easily, it makes good sense to take rest periods or breaks more frequently. Changes in vision usually begin in the forties or fifties, hearing loss should be checked out before it causes us to avoid social activities. Good nutrition, lots of healthful exercise, dedication to continued learning, and productive activity will help keep us ageless!

Question: I believe I'm allergic to exercise. I have tried videotapes and a few mechanical gadgets. Doesn't all the work I do around the house and yard give me plenty of exercise?

- Fifteen minutes of aerobic exercise each day reduces our risk of coronary artery disease by over 90 percent. Aerobic exercise is the kind of exercise that keeps you moving, gets you breathing, and raises your pulse. Walking, swimming laps at the pool, and even doing some yard tasks will certainly provide aerobic exercise. Brisk walking is the choice of most people because it gets us out of the house and, once indulged in regularly, becomes almost addictive. If you are not now doing aerobic exercise and wish to start, consult your doctor and have a good physical.

Question: I feel tied to my pill bottles these days. I take three different pills every day for blood pressure, arthritis, and hormone replacement. Is this an excessive amount of medication?

- No, not at all. Most older adults average four medications daily. But we do need to take all medications under a doctor's supervision. We also need to ask about over-the-counter medicines we may add at times. For example, some time-release cold capsules should not be taken with blood pressure medication. Ask the pharmacist's advice before adding an over-the-counter remedy to your prescription medicine.

- In Dr. Mark Beer's book, *Aging in Good Health*, the chapter on medications includes a chart of those that present special risks for older adults. The list includes "anticholinergic medications" that can disrupt the proper functioning of the bladder, colon, heart, blood vessels, eyes, and mouth. There is also a chart of medical conditions which can be made worse by certain prescription drugs. For instance, dehydration from flu can be worsened by the diuretics prescribed for treatment of high blood pressure.

Question: How necessary are flu shots every fall?

- Very necessary. While many medications are overused, vaccine for flu shots and vaccine for pneumonia are underused. Flu viruses change every year and the vaccines are carefully adjusted to counter the most common ones. A pneumonia shot may only be needed once in a lifetime since it remains potent once given. Flu and pneumonia vaccines can save the lives of older adults.

Question: Back problems and arthritis pain are my only real problems, and I find most of my friends complaining of these same conditions. Are these problems treatable?

- Osteoporosis, which is loss of bone density, can be an underlying cause of many back problems. Men are not as likely to be troubled by osteoporosis as women. However unfair it may seem, women begin to lose bone mass at twice the normal rate following menopause. While calcium-rich diets help in younger people, hormone therapy seems much more effective in older women.

- Arthritis is inflammation of the joints, and degenerative arthritis is a disease of old age. Pain is also caused by the loss of cartilage Surgery and replacement of the worn joint can be effective in cases where pain is severe. Nonsteroidal anti-inflammatory drugs such as aspirin are generally considered best for reducing inflammation and controlling pain. Exercise is an essential therapy for arthritis, particularly the water exercises taught by the National Arthritis Foundation. A gentle exercise that originated in China, tai chi, combines meditation and slow but effective body movement. Classes can be found in large cities, and community education can probably arrange for training classes in smaller communities.

Question: As I get older, I have more discomfort after eating and more problems with constipation than when I was younger. What's happening, and can I do something about it?

- Changes in the parasympathetic nervous system can change the way in which food moves through the upper and lower gastrointestinal tract. There are four other likely reasons for constipation: medications, particularly narcotic painkillers; medical conditions affecting the gastrointestinal system; lack of exercise; and a low-fiber diet. It is simple to increase fiber in the diet by adding plenty of fruits and vegetables, whole bran cereals, and Metamucil.

■ Reflux or regurgitation after eating a big meal means that the contents of the stomach move back into the esophagus, the tube connecting the mouth to the stomach. Although a burning sensation is the most common symptom, sometimes it is accompanied by chest pain, which can mimic a heart attack. For lack of a better general name, doctors call this presbyesophagus (presby means old) but no one really understands why it occurs. Doctors recommend eating slowly, chewing food well, moistening it by drinking plenty of water, and avoiding anticholinergic medications that slow the contractions of the esophagus. Reducing acidity with Tums or other medications is all right as a temporary measure, but an upper GI exam may be needed.

Question: I read and hear that people remain sexually active into their seventies and eighties. I'm a woman in my late sixties, and I have not maintained this interest. Is there something wrong with me?

■ In women, menopause affects levels of estrogen and progesterone, but it does not affect underlying sexuality. However, the linings of both the vagina and the urethra become thinner and dryer, and a condition called atrophic vaginitis can make intercourse painful. Medications are available to treat this condition.

■ Similarly, in men, testosterone levels decline with age, but this may have minimal effect on sexual interest or function. However, in combination with certain illnesses and some medications, it can cause impotence.

■ Finding a doctor with whom you can comfortably discuss these questions and possible solutions is important to you and your partner.

18 Coping with our health care system

In this exercise, the group will hear one retired couple's true health care experiences. They will follow the couple through four phases of knee replacement surgery: 1) decisions and choices, 2) preparations, 3) hospitalization, and 4) recovery.

Objectives

To be more aware of choices available when facing surgery.

To better understand the financial coverage available from Medicare.

To be cognizant of the need for supplemental insurance.

To be alert to the need for an advocate while hospitalized.

To be better able to choose between a nursing facility or home care during recovery.

Group size

Up to 40.

Time

$1-\frac{1}{4}$ hours.

Materials

One copy of each of the four sections of **Hank and Sally's adventure in health care**; four current copies of *Medicare: What It Covers, What It Doesn't*; easel pad and markers.

Information about Medicare

When adults are eligible for Social Security, they also become eligible for Medicare, the federal health insurance program. Medicare does not cover all your medical expenses. (Actually it pays less than half of the total health bill for retired seniors.)

Part A of Medicare, the hospital insurance, pays part of the costs of hospital care, limited care in a certified nursing facility, home health care, and hospice care. No premium is required for Part A, but you will need to pay part of the costs and a deductible of $716 before Medicare takes over. If you carry supplemental insurance, it will usually cover this deductible.

Part B, medical insurance, covers physician services, outpatient care, and lab services. The monthly premium for Part B may be deducted from your Social Security check. Additionally you must pay an annual deductible of $100 plus 20 percent of the amount Medicare approves for each of your medical bills. If your doctor's fee is greater than the approved amount (the Medicare assignment fee) your supplemental insurance must pick up the additional amount, or you must pay it. (1995 *Medicare: What It Covers, What It Doesn't*, a publication of AARP.)

The information above was current in 1995. Details of Medicare coverage change, so each year the American Association of Retired Persons, AARP, publishes an updated explanation of Medicare benefits. For a copy of this publication, write to:

AARP Fulfillment
601 E Street N.W.
Washington, DC 20049

Process

1. Introduce the session to participants with the following comments:

   ■ Anyone who has recently visited or been a patient in a regional health center that provides diagnostic and hospital services for a large geographic area will be impressed by our modern health care system. The buildings, equipment, array of specialists and other trained personnel, and the stories of the lifesaving feats that have been accomplished help us understand, at least in part, our huge national bill for health care services.

   ■ It is clear to most of us that our health care system is far too complex. Even bills from our family physician are bewildering. Some of us find the system so intimidating that we stay away from the doctor as much as possible and even put off needed hospitalization.

2. Introduce Hank and Sally's story:

   ■ Today, we are going to talk about one older couple's experiences with surgery. I will read the introduction to **Hank and Sally's adventure in health care**, and then we'll form four groups for discussion of the decisions and choices that Hank and Sally made, the preparations that preceded surgery, Hank's hospitalization, and his recovery.

3. Read the introduction to Hank and Sally's story, which begins on page 114.

4. Form four small groups. Distribute one section of Hank and Sally's four-part story to each group and give the following instructions:

   ➤ Choose a spokesperson and a recorder for your group. The spokesperson will read one section of the story aloud. The recorder will take notes on the discussion that follows. When we reconvene the entire group, your spokesperson will share a condensed version of your part of the story along with insights from your group's discussion.

➤ After listening to the story, make any suggestions you believe might be helpful to Hank and Sally at this particular stage of the process they are going through. Your personal experiences with the health care system may provide good suggestions. Try not to get stuck on frustrations; emphasize techniques that you have found work well. Take about 20 minutes for this discussion.

5. Reconvene the whole group and have each of the four groups summarize their section of the story and make comments and suggestions.

6. Following the reports, close with these additional facts:

- Medicaid provides health coverage for individuals with low incomes. It is not necessary to have supplemental insurance if you are enrolled in Medicaid, which is a joint federal and state program. Most Medicare beneficiaries do not qualify for Medicaid until they "spend down" their assets. States vary in their policies to prevent "spousal impoverishment." Usually the home and a portion of assets can be retained.

- You will have fewer problems if your physician will accept "the assignment fee" approved by Medicare. In this case, patients will be responsible for paying only 20 percent of the physician's fee.

- Your local Social Security office has a statewide physician's directory. Use it to determine whether your doctor accepts the assignment fee.

- Supplemental insurance advertised as "Medigap" must by law offer standardized coverage. This insurance offers ten different coverage plans at varying costs.

These plans, identified by the letters A through J, are described in AARP's publication.

■ When you become eligible for Social Security, Medicare coverage is not automatic. You must apply for it. When you enroll, you will receive a copy of the Medicare Handbook.

Hank and Sally's adventure in health care

Introduction:

Their neighborhood's common road was just under a mile in circumference, and it was beautifully decked out on this sunny July morning with hundreds of wild daisies and some of June's remaining wild roses. But hiking had ceased to be fun this year, Sally reflected. Hank was in too much pain to be walking even this much loved mile. He stubbornly insisted, however, that he needed the exercise.

Osteoarthritis had started in Hank's knee when he was in his midfifties, and now ten years later had progressed to the point that he often need a cane to walk and had received a disability sign for his car. Some five years ago, the doctors said his knee joint should be replaced but that Hank must determine when surgery should be done. At that time, Hank wasn't ready. The main consideration in his doctor's view was that the pain be controlled well enough with medication that it would not interfere with sleep or cause other health problems.

Now seeing his slow gait and the pain lines in his face, Sally asked, "Hank, isn't it time? Haven't you suffered enough?"

"I guess so. I've been holding out because I want the new knee to last till I'm ninety-three," Hank said with a grin. "But when you can't hike on a day like this, maybe it is time."

As Hank and Sally walked down the driveway to their retirement home on the lakeshore, they both felt the sense of thanksgiving and serenity their home always provided. Completed just two years ago, the winterized addition to their summer cabin had been turned into a well-planned home for the years ahead. The car could be driven right to the ground-level deck, and there were no steps to climb. Wide doorways allowed convenient access. Bedroom and bath were close together, and a walk-in shower and separate tub gave choices for convenient bathing.

"We're going to do just fine," Sally said as they entered the house.

"Once we get the finances figured out," Hank added, but thought to himself, "With Medicare, supplemental insurance, and no mortgage, we should do okay."

©1997 Whole Person Press 210 W Michigan Duluth MN 55802   (800) 247-6789

Part I. Decisions and choices

Hank visited his local physician, Dr. Howard, just a few days later, on July 15. "Doc, I've decided to go ahead with the knee replacement surgery. It's not that the pain is any worse. It's the walking. Getting around in general is getting really tough."

"I know, Hank. I've wondered how you could hold out so long. You're in good health, so this is an ideal time to have surgery."

"I want a good surgeon to do my knee. I'm willing to go to the Mayo Clinic if necessary. Who do you suggest?" Dr. Howard strongly recommended Duluth's medical complex. "It would be easier for you and your wife to have the shorter travel distance. And there are expert orthopedic surgeons in Duluth who do many of these surgeries every year." Dr. Howard named four, telling Hank a bit about each. Then he said, "Personally I guess I would put Dr. Bob Stevens at the top of my list. He took care of my wife, Ann, last winter, repairing an arm broken badly in a skiing accident. It was a tricky job to fix, but it is now as good as new."

The personal experience was the clincher with Hank. "I'd like to talk to Dr. Stevens and ask him some questions."

Early in August, Hank drove to the clinic in Duluth and met an energetic, very busy, very convincing young surgeon whom Hank soon decided he liked and trusted. Looking over the X-rays of Hank's knee, there was good give and take in their conversation. Dr. Stevens explained the procedure, and Hank asked questions. Finally Hank asked, "Are you a good surgeon?"

Dr. Stevens looked a bit surprised, then he said very seriously, "Yes, I am. Presently I have more surgery patients for knees and hip joints than any of my colleagues. My patients do well with me, and I'm proud of that."

So the date was set for October 29th. Hank learned that the surgeon's fee would be approximately $5,000.

Part II. Preparations

Once the surgery date had been set, Hank and Sally embarked on an endless list of things to do. Getting used to living without the potent pain medication he'd been taking for five years was the first hurdle. Hank's pain medicine was also a blood thinner, so with surgery coming up, he had to stop it well in advance.

The fall house and yard chores needed to be started early. Completing them would require plenty of rest periods and maybe some hired help. Sally always helped, but a back problem limited her physical activities. She did, however, learn to fill the car's gas tank, something she said she ought to have learned much earlier.

"Thank heaven you're a good, reliable driver!" Hank commented. "You're going to be doing all the driving for a couple of months after my surgery."

By looking at the materials they'd collected on Medicare coverage and on their own supplemental insurance, they learned the following: supplemental insurance Plan H would cover the portion of the doctor's fee exceeding the amount allowed by Medicare. It would also pay the $716 Part A deductible after which Medicare pays almost all hospital expenses for up to sixty days. Medicare also pays for at least part of the physical therapy needed after surgery and for all the medications given in the hospital.

One afternoon, Sally suddenly said, "Hank, you'll need a walker and crutches when you come home. Where will we get them?"

"Hey, I'll give the county public health office a call and ask where I could rent some." Hank made the call and minutes later was back smiling. "They have walkers and crutches to loan out without charge. I can pick them up early so I can try them out before I go in for surgery."

In early October, Hank had a complete physical and final lab tests. In case a transfusion was needed, two units of blood were drawn and banked. Surgery was scheduled for October 29.

Part III. Hospitalization

It was 10:00 P.M. on November 4. Sally's thoughts were in turmoil. She had left Hank's hospital room after another long day at his bedside. Today was the fifth day of Hank's hospitalization. The surgery had gone very well. On the knee extension machine, he'd reached a bend of ninety degrees. But Hank was decidedly not himself. He was unable to eat, had severe bouts of hiccups, and couldn't stay awake. Worst of all, Sally could not get anyone's attention about her concern. Dr. Stevens had left for a medical conference two days after Hank's surgery, leaving Hank in the care of his colleagues. They came in every morning and looked at Hank's chart and his incision, but they had never met him prior to the operation.

Sally had voiced her concern to the nurses, but they gave her the stock answers, "Patients often have trouble eating after surgery," or "He is most likely sleepy from pain medication."

As she got ready for bed that fifth night, Sally felt acute concern and the sense that an injustice was being done. "I've had enough!" she said out loud. "Hank can't stand up for himself. I have to!"

The next morning, Sally gave a handwritten letter to the supervising nurse. In it, she described Hank's troubling symptoms and wrote, "My husband is not getting better, he is getting weaker. I want an internist to look at him immediately." Sally told the nurse that she wanted the letter placed with her husband's chart and called to the attention of his doctors.

By that afternoon an internist examined Hank and found a serious viral infection in his esophagus. Treatment was started and produced results almost immediately. On the tenth day Hank had recovered enough to go home. What should have been a five- to seven-day hospital stay had lasted almost twice as long, and Hank went home without as much vigor and energy as they had hoped. As they drove the familiar road, Hank said, "Everyone needs a family member or some advocate with them when they're hospitalized for surgery."

©1997 Whole Person Press 210 W Michigan Duluth MN 55802   (800) 247-6789

Part IV. Recovery

Although Medicare will pay for recovery time in a nursing facility, home is definitely the place to recover if at all possible.

Hank looked forward to home-cooked food, his king-size bed, and his handy bathroom and walk-in shower. He knew how to care for his incision and how to continue his exercises.

Sally was sure she could handle the caregiving and the household and chauffeuring jobs. But she was not quite prepared for how tired she got by the end of the day. She would have willingly taken herself off to the second bedroom by 8:00 P.M., but she rarely made it before 10:00 P.M.

Recovery progressed well. The only gloomy notes were the hospital and clinic bills, which seemed to arrive daily. Hank and Sally were meticulous about paying their debts on time. Since most of these envelopes contained statements like, "Not a Bill" or "A bill has been submitted to your insurance carrier" or "total due" or "your total responsibility," they had no way of knowing what they really owed. One time they took "Your total responsibility" seriously and sent in the amount. Shortly thereafter, they received a return check for the same amount. This was a waste of time and postage, and it created a new frustration.

Because a clerical mistake had also been made when Hank's account was established, the supplemental bill for Hank's care was sent to the wrong insurer.

One day a card arrived from the clinic. "Attention Patient" it began. It went on to explain that from then on the clinic would submit claims to all insurance sources BEFORE submitting a bill to the patient. Furthermore, the bill would show per item what was paid by Medicare and by supplemental insurance. It would finally be possible to know what was left to be paid by the patient.

"Alleluia, on behalf of us and of all the other bewildered users of health services. Maybe we'll get clarification at last!" Hank fervently commented.

19 The indispensable woman

In this exercise, a story is used to illustrate how all-encompassing a cause or retirement career can become. Even in retirement, it's important to maintain a balanced schedule that includes purposeful work, consideration for one's spouse, time to maintain a healthy lifestyle, and fun and recreation.

Objectives

To understand that commitment to a cause must be controlled and kept in balance.

To realize that we must be the best caretakers of our own health.

To recognize that the happiness and concerns of our spouse must be considered.

To understand that sharing responsibility is a talent to cultivate.

Group size

Unlimited.

Time

30–40 minutes.

Materials

Easel pad and markers.

Process

1. Introduce the exercise to participants by presenting the following comments:

   - One of the most stimulating and invigorating things retirees can do is find a cause and work for it.

- However, there are times when people can get carried away by a cause.

- There are also times when the sense of power such jobs bring can cloud our judgment. The story you are about to hear illustrates such a case.

2. Read or have one of the participants read aloud **The indispensable woman**, which is printed on pages 122–24.

3. If the group has more than ten members, print the questions that follow on the easel pad and, after reading the story, form small groups for discussion. Otherwise, discuss the questions with the whole group.

   ✔ Must Helen choose between health and her cause?

   ✔ What role should her husband play in her choice?

   ✔ Did Dr. O'Brien lay out the health risks sufficiently?

   ✔ Assuming Pamela knew of Helen's health problems, should she have encouraged Helen to take over as chairperson of the commission?

   ✔ Is it really necessary for Helen to accept so much responsibility?

   ✔ What advice would you give Helen if you could speak to her very frankly? Should she be the "indispensable woman?"

   ✔ Is there any cause you might get into which would put you in a similar situation?

4. Summarize the discussion in your own words or use the following ideas:

   - In a good marriage, both partners should have an equal say in the lifestyle they adopt in retirement. This story leads us to suspect that Douglas has not been treated fairly.

   - Helen does not realize that she is also not playing fair

with fellow commission members. They would not have been appointed if they weren't effective workers. If Helen assumes too much power, she will not carry out her real responsibility as chairperson, which is to build a strong decision-making group.

5. Conclude by asking participants to propose a best-case and a worst-case scenario for Helen one year after the events of this story.

The indispensable woman

Garbed in a hospital gown which barely covered her plump frame, Helen Moore awaited her doctor in the clinic's examining room. She felt tense and frustrated because she was missing a meeting in the mayor's office. As a member of the planning committee for the new senior center, she wanted to be there more than anywhere in the world at this moment.

A metallic click announced Dr. O'Brien's arrival followed by his cheery "Hi, Helen. How have you been?" It was her doctor's stock question at all her bimonthly appointments. As always, Helen gave her stock answer, "Fine."

But Helen was not fine. She was seventy-two, a diabetic, and she had a driving conviction that she alone could make the Holmes County Aging Program the best in the nation. As vice-chairperson of the Commission on Aging, she attended four or five meetings a week, and her busy schedule tended to make her careless about her diet.

"Any problems?" asked Dr. O'Brien, placing his stethoscope to listen to her heart and lungs, while wondering, as he always did, how he could make Helen understand that she was no longer fifty, and she should start taking better care of herself.

"Oh, I get a bit tired, but I'm really fine." Helen had chosen to ignore the nurse's exclamation of alarm when she took Helen's blood pressure. Helen half-hoped Dr. O'Brien would forget to take it again.

But he did not forget. "Maggie says your blood pressure is up.

Let's see." A moment of silence as he adjusted the cuff and raised the pressure. An alarmed whistle was his next response. "What have you been up to Helen? It is up. Considerably up!"

"Well, there were lots of meetings this month. We are really down to the wire on planning the senior center. But this is my life. I love what I do. I'd be a basket case if I sat around home all day."

Dr. O'Brien folded his arms and stood looking at her. "Yes, I know you enjoy what you are doing. You have great commitment; you also have diabetes and high blood pressure. Cut down on the running around and get more rest. I'm going to increase your medication and make an appointment for you with Dr. Jane Collins for biofeedback sessions. Make an appointment to see me again next week."

As Helen pulled into the driveway of her home, her husband, Douglas, shut off the lawn mower and came over to help her with several bags of groceries. "Well, what did the doctor have to say?" he asked.

"Dr. O'Brien says I'm fine except for a little elevation in my blood pressure."

"He didn't ground you? I thought for sure he would." Douglas looked surprised and dismayed.

"Nobody's grounding me!" Helen announced vehemently. "Any calls?"

"Yes, Pamela Neville called. She said it was important. She wants you to call her either at the office or at home. What are you, the indispensable woman?"

"I'll try her right away. Then how about my treating you to supper out tonight for doing such a good job on the lawn?" Helen patted her husband's arm affectionately as they went up the front steps.

She put her grocery bag and purse on a hall chair, noting with approval that Douglas had vacuumed and tidied up. She dialed Pamela's office number from memory. "Hello, Pamela, this is Helen. What's up?"

Pamela Neville's soft voice belied a controlled, organized, and uncompromising personality. She had served as director of the County Aging Program for five years, never failing to keep it on top of the county's funding agenda.

"I'm glad you called, Helen. I have news for you. John Tonzack has decided to resign the chairmanship of the commission immediately. He has been thinking about it for awhile as you know. As our vice-chairperson, you are in line to take over. You would make a wonderful chairperson, but I know how busy you are already. Can you accept this added work and responsibility?"

Helen was silent for a moment. She had a mental image of Dr. O'Brien shaking his head. Then all her dreams of wielding the gavel at commission meetings triumphed.

"I surely can accept and I do! When do I come in to start planning the agenda for the next commission meeting. Let me see, it's a week from Wednesday, isn't it?"

20 Things of the spirit

Traditional forms of religious worship give many people ways in which to express their spirituality. Those who do not claim a religious faith also have a spiritual side to their being. In this exercise, participants will explore a variety of spiritual experiences through creative writing. The discussion that follows will encourage them to continue thinking about things of the spirit.

Objectives

To be more aware of the settings and times when our spiritual self is recognized.

To begin or continue a search for spiritual experiences.

To share perceptions of spirit with family and friends.

To become eager to explore and enjoy the variety of spiritual perceptions entering our lives.

Group size

20–30 participants.

Time

30–40 minutes.

Materials

Easel pad and markers; paper and pencils.

☞ *The activities in this exercise can be used with any group, but the introductory comments may need to be adapted for specific groups.*

Process

Introduce the concept of spirituality by making the following points, adapting them as needed for your group:

- Spirituality is our inner source of courage, healing, love, creativity, and wisdom.

- Contact with our spiritual self often arrives without effort. Momentary perceptions come with prayer, mantras, daydreaming, imagining, running, star gazing, and many other mind-freeing activities. The spiritual self is universal in humans. Could it be our soul?

- To encourage the inner self to take over, a person needs to be playful, to engage in unstructured activities, and to feel secure enough to "let go."

- The two activities we will engage in during this session are designed to allow this to happen.

☞ *Music played softly in the background may help people relax and participate more freely in these activities.*

Part A. Moments in touch

1. Introduce the first activity by making some of the following comments about spirituality:

- People feel in touch with the spiritual side of themselves, their inner self, in a variety of settings while engaging in many different activities.

- Some people will find that spiritual state of being while engaged in prayer, others while engrossed by the beauty of nature, still others while listening to music or while involved in a loving relationship or an emotional crisis.

- The common thread that allows us to respond from the depths of our being is the freedom that comes from letting go and no longer monitoring our thoughts and actions.

- By taking a few moments to recall some of those special moments and then by sharing them with others, we can begin to recognize how "letting go" enhances the spirit within us.

2. Distribute paper and pencils and provide the following instructions. Read each one very slowly and pause after each phrase:

➤ Close your eyes; lean back in your chair; take a few deep, relaxing breaths; and in your imagination, wander back through your life and relive a time when you were truly in touch with your inner self—with your deepest spirit.

➤ Don't feel pressured to find great significance in these images; whatever they may be, just let them play through your mind.

➤ As you recall the circumstances and your feelings, make a few notes about the experience on your paper.

➤ Then close your eyes again, and another experience may come to mind.

3. After 5 minutes, or when it appears that most people have written a few words, ask participants to share their memories. List them on the easel pad and ask for comments about similarities and differences. Then encourage the group to discuss how they might become more open to these experiences.

Part B. Dialogue with yourself as a child

1. Introduce the activity with the following comments:

■ Young children tend to be imaginative and spontaneous. They don't analyze their thoughts, words, and actions the way that adults do.

■ To recover some of that spontaneity, we will now take a few minutes to dialogue with that child each of us once was.

2. Form groups of four to six participants. It is best if they sit around small tables. Provide the following instructions, which should be read slowly, pausing after each phrase:

➤ Close your eyes; lean back; relax; and begin to imagine yourself as a five-year-old child. Take a moment to make the image real, picturing yourself in a special place, engaged in an activity you enjoy.

➤ Add yourself as an adult to the scene you are imagining. Perhaps you are pushing your five-year-old self on a swing, reading a book together, or playing with a favorite toy.

➤ Now begin a conversation between your five-year-old self and your adult self. Do you have a question to ask yourself as a child? Would your five-year-old self like to ask something of your adult self? Be playful and creative.

➤ As the conversation develops, begin to write what you are saying and what you are feeling—as a child and also as an adult. Don't seek for deep insights; don't analyze or describe; just experience and record.

➤ Remember that this is a dialogue with yourself at two different points in time. Play both sides of it to the hilt, guided by your spiritual self rather than by rules and standards of writing.

3. At the end of 5 minutes, or when most people have written at least a few words, conclude the writing and lead a discussion of the process, asking participants whether they were surprised by their thoughts and feelings.

   ☞ In this exercise, the discussion can become rather emotional. Tears are often seen in participants' eyes as they view their childhood in this different light. If *you are not a trained psychologist, it would be well to calmly close the session at this stage.*

4. In summary, ask participants to share some of their insights. The following questions may help with that process:

✔ Which exercise put you more in touch with your inner self?

✔ In what ways does spirituality give you a sense of direction for your life?

✔ How has your spirituality helped you face problems associated with work, family, pain, illness, death, or other issues?

✔ In what ways do we starve our spiritual self?

✔ Are you ever surprised to have a totally free weekend? When you do, what spiritual journeys could you choose to take?

Variations

■ As an alternative or in addition to the dialogue with yourself, the group could have fun with one or both of the following options:

A dialogue between yourself at your present age and your spouse at age five.

A dialogue between yourself at age five and your grandfather or grandmother.

21 Thinking of death

Older adults often play peek-a-boo with thoughts about death. We cover our eyes because we don't want to see, yet we peek because we do want to see. In this nonthreatening exercise, participants will explore the manner in which they would want to be informed by a physician about a terminal illness.

Objectives

To view death in a rational way.

To bring our basic values into our thought processes about the end of life.

To be more willing to talk to others about the "end game" faced by everyone.

To encourage a willingness to make plans for the contingencies of later life.

To see death from our own perspective as well as that of others, such as a spouse, doctor, spiritual leader, or friend.

To understand some of the different ways in which older adults view death.

Group size

Unlimited.

Time

Up to 1 hour with groups of 10–20 participants; allow additional time for larger groups.

Materials

Easel pad and markers; pencils; **Prognosis: terminal** worksheet.

Process

1. Introduce the exercise in your own words or by using some of the comments that follow. To set the stage for a serious, but not morbid, discussion, personalize the introduction by drawing from your own experience.

   ■ As we age, death appears different than it did when we were children or young adults.

   ■ If we read the obituaries daily, it's because we are losing friends, relatives, and acquaintances. Those of us who travel during the year are likely, on our return, to find that someone we knew died while we were gone.

   ■ Although we might feel a little anxious thinking about death, today we'll have a chance to talk about our concerns as we consider how we would like to be informed about a terminal illness.

2. Read the following scenario to the group.

   Imagine yourself in this situation. One week ago, you had a complete physical examination. Upon reviewing the results of the laboratory tests, your doctor realized that you have a terminal illness. The facts about your illness and its prognosis are as follows:

   ■ *You have no more than one year to live, most likely just five to seven months. No medications or other treatments are known to help.*

   ■ *There will be little pain or incapacity prior to the last month. Until that time, you should be able to live a fairly normal life.*

   ■ *Only minor changes in your appearance are to be expected.*

   ■ *The costs of medical care during the final month will be moderate.*

   ■ *Your illness is not contagious.*

©1997 Whole Person Press 210 W Michigan Duluth MN 55802   (800) 247-6789

3. Distribute the **Prognosis: terminal** worksheet to participants. Allow 5 minutes for participants to read the instructions and complete the worksheet, placing their rankings in the column headed "Individual."

4. Following completion of the worksheet, form groups of 4–6 participants. When possible, form the groups by age, placing people in their fifties in one group, those in their sixties in another, and so on. Ask participants, within their groups, to try to come to a consensus on their rankings. Offer the following suggestions for consensus building:

   ➤ Avoid arguing emotionally for your original ranking. Use logic and respect the logic of others.

   ➤ Listen to the ideas and feelings of other group members. They may have more information or experiences that are different from yours.

   ➤ Don't give in just to reach agreement. Support your own ideas and share the reasons for any doubts you have.

   ➤ Do not rely on majority rule. Recognize that partial agreement may be acceptable when decisions are made on the basis of facts, logic, and feelings.

5. After 15 minutes, ask participants to enter the group's rankings on their worksheet in the column headed "Group."

6. Reconvene the group and ask for participants' insights. The following questions may be used to elicit discussion.

   ✔ Which of the methods listed was the very best way for the doctor to communicate this bad news?

   ✔ Is there a better way that was not listed?

   ✔ Which was the worst way?

   ✔ Why is it so difficult to talk about death with a spouse,

family member, friend, doctor, or even a spiritual advisor?

✔ Assuming that talking about death is better than "holding it in," how could this be made easier?

7. Encourage participants to begin discussing these issues with people who are important to them. You may share the following story with the group if you want to illustrate the benefits of dealing openly with death.

Patti Couture died at age forty-one on August 23, 1995. She knew that her cancer was terminal. Two weeks before her death she said to her husband, "When you see an eagle soaring, think of me. That will be my soul."

Early in the year, Patti had made a list of "things I always wanted to do but never did." She shared the list with family and friends and did some of the things before her death.

Most of us are not as aware of the nearness of death, but Patti's words and life-loving spirit left a message. She said, "Death is going to come for all of us. I think it's a lot better to laugh than to cry."

Variations

■ If you have less than an hour available, combine the processes described in steps 4–6 and complete them with the entire group.

■ If participants want to continue this discussion, **Life and Death Questions** in Volume 2 of *Structured Exercises in Wellness Promotion* (available from Whole Person Associates) provides another thought-provoking exercise.

Prognosis: terminal

Seven ways in which a doctor could communicate the news of your approaching death are listed below. Rank them from 1 to 7 according to the way you believe the diagnosis should be given to you. In the column headed "Individual," give a rating of "1" to the way you prefer, a "2" to the next preferred, and so on.

Individual Group

1. I'd like to receive very little information until the last month when I start to become incapacitated. Then I'd like a complete report. _____ _____

2. I don't want to discuss my disease or the prognosis, but the doctor should meet with my family so they are aware of the consequences of my illness. _____ _____

3. I prefer a straightforward explanation of my disease and the expectation that I will die within one year. _____ _____

4. I think the doctor should talk first with my family and my spiritual advisor, and they should, together, decide how much I should be told. _____ _____

5. I don't think the doctor should offer any information about this terminal illness unless I specifically insist on hearing it. _____ _____

6. I believe the doctor should explain the disease and the prognosis but should offer some hope for cure or remission even if that is not realistic. _____ _____

7. I think the doctor should explain the disease but lie about the prognosis, providing only the best recovery scenario. _____ _____

22 The last year of life

In this exercise participants will summarize their philosophy of life in a short statement and will answer the question: What would I do if I had but one year to live?

Objectives

To integrate our basic philosophy of life into plans for the approach of death.

To face death with a better self-understanding and to bring a more objective closure to life.

Group size

5–20 people who participated in the previous exercise and who want to continue the discussion.

Time

Up to 1 hour.

Materials

Paper and pencils.

☞ *Leaders should complete the writing portion of this exercise themselves before presenting the exercise to groups.*

Process

1. Introduce the exercise by commenting on the discussion that took place during the previous session and on the fact that the people assembled for this session have chosen to participate because they were interested in continuing to discuss the end of life.

2. Distribute paper and pencils and provide the following instructions:

   ➤ Today, you will have a chance to think about the

plans you would make if this were your last year of life. To decide how to live that final year, it's essential to stop and think about what's really important to you. To help you do this, write a paragraph or two on your philosophy of life. Consider your basic beliefs about religion, truth, hope, faith, wisdom, aesthetics, and values. Take about 10 minutes for this step.

➤ After you've finished your statement of belief, continue by answering this question: If you learned that you had a terminal illness and were expected to live less than a year, what would you plan for your last year of life?

3. After most people have finished writing, begin a discussion of their statements. You may want to ask some of the following questions:

✔ In what way does your philosophy of life dictate how you approach death?

✔ In what ways were your plans for your last year affected by the fact that you just finished writing out your philosophy of life?

✔ Was it difficult for you to be realistic in planning for the last year of your life?

✔ Which things are hardest to imagine doing for the very last time?

✔ In what ways did factors such as your religious beliefs, your financial situation, previous resolutions that you have not yet fulfilled, and concern for others enter into your thinking?

4. It may be difficult to draw the discussion to a conclusion, so you should plan for closure in advance. You might summarize by saying that, for each of us, the

present year could be our last year, so we should be sure that every year reflects our philosophy of life.

Variation

- If the group is truly and openly involved in this exercise, they might find it interesting and enlightening to write their own obituaries.

23 Promise yourself good choices

Our decisions are influenced by internal forces such as interests and values and by external forces such as finances and health. By analyzing several recently made decisions, participants will recognize these forces and consider the impact they will have on retirement decisions yet to come.

Objectives

To develop a framework for making sound retirement choices.

To clarify the impact of internal and external factors on our retirement.

To determine which factors are most satisfying personally.

To continually reevaluate long-term retirement decisions.

Group size

Up to 50.

Time

40–70 minutes.

Materials

Paper and pencils; easel pad and markers.

Process

1. Introduce the concept of retirement choices by asking participants, as you list them on the easel pad, to call out some of the choices they either anticipate making or have already made.

2. Distribute paper and pencils to each participant and present the following instructions:

➤ List three decisions you made in the past ten years that turned out to be good choices. They need not be related to retirement.

➤ Following each decision, explain how you made it and why you believe it was a good choice.

➤ Turn the paper over and on the back list three specific decisions related to retirement that you must make during the next ten years.

➤ After each item, suggest what you can do to increase the chance that this decision will be a good one. If you are unsure about this, leave it blank for later review by the group.

3. After 15 minutes, or when most participants seem to be done writing, present the concept of internal and external forces that influence our decisions, making some of the following points:

■ We use the phrase "free choice," but our choices are actually determined, or at least influenced, by a number of forces, both internal and external.

■ Internal forces include deeply held values and beliefs, feelings of love or hate, talents and skills, and casual or intense interests.

■ External factors include health, money, power, residence, and relationships.

■ The internal forces that affect our decisions may seem to be more significant. Yet external forces are also important. For example, if we want to give freely and volunteer generous amounts of time to a cause, we must have the financial resources to make this possible.

4. Ask each participant to review the six decisions they

wrote about, identifying those decisions as being influenced by internal, external, or joint forces.

5. Ask participants to share with the group the decisions on their lists that they weren't sure how to make. Write those items on the left side of the easel pad. If none are offered, ask individuals to volunteer examples of difficult retirement decisions.

6. To the right of the list, head two columns with the words external forces and internal forces. See the layout below with one example.

Difficult choices	External forces	Internal forces
Leaving job	No work to do	Feelings of loss
	No structure to days	Real interests
	No required activities	Worries about
	Loss of peers	handling freedom
		Lack of knowledge

7. If you need more examples than participants provide, consider how to deal with opportunities for mobility, financial changes, more free time, and physical aging.

8. After participating in this process, participants will be more aware of how they can analyze their choices by considering the external and internal forces that influence them. Conclude the session by asking the group whether they prefer to base their decisions on internal or external forces. Do not ignore the potential for both forces to play a part in a single decision.

Variation

- If you have enough time, you may want to form small groups for the discussion in step 5.

Assessing yourself

24 Whole person retirement

Wisely chosen activities can improve the quality of life during retirement years. In this exercise, participants will evaluate their current physical, mental, spiritual, social, and civic activities and will consider the multitude of options available to them.

Objectives

To become more aware of the type of activities which are open to us and in which we can take part.

To determine how our activities and interests compare to those of others in the group.

To make intelligent choices about activities that will lead to personal growth.

Group size

Unlimited.

Time

40–50 minutes.

Materials

Easel pad and markers; pencils; small slips of paper; **How active am I?** worksheets.

Process

1. Introduce the benefits of an active retirement by drawing from your own experience or by making some of the following comments:

   ■ Studies have shown that people who remain physically and mentally active during their retirement years tend to be healthy and happy.

- Although some people focus exclusively on one area of life—physical, mental, spiritual, social, or civic—a whole person approach to life can provide valuable balance. For example, retirees who immerse themselves in civic ventures, allowing no time for regular physical activity, may find that the health problems that come with a sedentary lifestyle will keep them from the civic work they love.

- If we engage in a variety of activities, we will have valuable options. For example, if we enjoy reading, we won't be bored when bad weather keeps us from hiking or socializing. If we have many friends, the loss of one won't leave us without companionship.

- The amount of activity that each person needs for optimal physical and mental health varies greatly. A weekly schedule that would overwhelm one person might leave another restless and understimulated.

2. Distribute the **How active am I?** worksheets and provide the following instructions:

➤ This worksheet, which is divided into five areas, will help you determine how active you are right now. If during the past month, you have participated in an activity at the level described, mark it with an X.

➤ This is not a contest. Having lots of X's isn't necessarily better than having few, but if you are honest with yourself, the worksheet will help you evaluate your lifestyle and decide whether you want to make any changes.

3. After participants are finished writing, distribute slips of paper and provide the following instructions:

➤ Add the X's in each section and write the section totals on your worksheet.

➤ Add the section totals to obtain a grand total. Write the

grand total on your worksheet and also write it on the slip of paper you received. Pass that paper to the front.

4. Ask one of the participants to sort the slips of paper, placing them in numerical order. As that is being done, list the numbers 1–20 in a column on the easel pad. Ask the person who sorted the slips of paper to call out the number of people who recorded 1 on their worksheet, and place that number next to the 1 on the easel pad. Continue down the column.

5. During the follow-up discussion explain that lots of activity is not necessarily best for everyone. Comment on the variations among individuals that you see reflected in the numbers on the easel pad. Questions similar to those that follow will help participants judge for themselves whether they are too active or not active enough, whether they have concentrated too much on one or two activities or might be engaged in a multitude of activities for the sole purpose of being busy.

✔ What is a proper balance among the five areas of activity listed? (physical, mental, spiritual, social, and civic)

✔ If your activities were concentrated in one or two areas, why do you think this is true?

✔ Are some of us more prone, because of our personalities, to spread our activities over several areas?

✔ How much does family background affect choices about involvement?

✔ What kinds of activities important to you have been left off the checklist? Do they fit within any of the five areas we considered?

✔ What new activities would you like to explore?

6. Conclude the session by encouraging participants to consider their body, mind, spirit, and relationships as they make decisions about retirement activities.

©1997 Whole Person Press 210 W Michigan Duluth MN 55802   (800) 247-6789

How active am I?

Physical activities
During the past month I have . . .

___ 1. Walked or run an average of two miles every day. (Do not count chores.)

___ 2. Taken part in organized physical activities such as exercise classes, dances, or sports once each week.

___ 3. Engaged in individual exercise at least five days each week.

___ 4. Exerted myself physically at least once each week in swimming, heavy work, or exercise.

Mental activities
During the past month I have . . .

___ 5. Played cards, chess, checkers, Trivial Pursuit, or other stimulating mental games.

___ 6. Attended at least one organized learning group. (religious study, adult class, business-sponsored classes, etc.)

___ 7. Discussed with knowledgeable persons how to solve or better understand a problem.

___ 8. Deliberately watched and listened to educational television and radio programs.

Spiritual activities
During the past month I have . . .

___ 9. Regularly made time to relax, meditate, dream, and engage in solitary experiences.

___10. Contemplated the natural world; relaxed in the mystery of the sunrise, sunset, or full moon;

became engrossed by clouds, waves, whispering leaves, or a rainbow.

___11. Taken time to commune with God in prayer, to read scripture, or to engage in compassionate conversation.

___12. Regularly backed away from overstimulation by work, media, and home to spend time alone.

Social activities
During the past month I have . . .

___13. Spent at least two half-days or evenings visiting with relatives, close friends, or neighbors.

___14. Stopped and chatted with people I know in stores, public buildings, on the street, or wherever I may have seen them.

___15. Shared at least two meals with friends.

___16. Attended at least one social event with friends.

Civic activities
During the past year I have . . .

___17. Written, phoned, or talked to at least one public official about local government issues.

___18. Been involved as a committee member or volunteer in a program for community improvement.

___19. Belonged to at least one club or organization involved in civic activities.

___20. Watched TV programs or read articles weekly that dealt with world problems and solutions.

Section totals

Physical	_____	Social	_____
Mental	_____	Civic	_____
Spiritual	_____	**TOTAL**	_____

25 Attitude adjustment

By developing role-plays that present positive and negative attitudes towards retirement, participants will better understand the importance of a good outlook as they respond to life changes.

Objectives

To recognize attitudes that make us appear positive or negative to ourselves or to our peers.

To rate our own retirement behavior in relation to that of others.

To think about retirement more positively.

To have more empathy with and understanding of those whose retirement behavior is different from our own.

Group size

Works well with up to 40.

Time

1 hour.

Materials

Exercise in choice cards; paper and pencils.

Process

1. Introduce the exercise to the group with the following comments:

   ■ Most retirement research completed prior to 1980 focused on problems of retirees. Because case studies concentrated on people found in nursing homes,

©1997 Whole Person Press 210 W Michigan Duluth MN 55802   (800) 247-6789

doctor's offices, and senior centers, they concluded that retirement was negative.

■ Recent research has studied successful retirees rather than the frail elderly. These studies developed a much more positive picture of retirement.

■ Many newly retired persons find themselves as busy as they were before they retired, but those who had an optimistic view of life prior to retirement are likely to fare better than those who were pessimistic.

■ People who are highly satisfied with life, substituting new activities for old ones, tend to have a positive retirement.

■ Those who just hold on and keep busy but shut out new experiences tend to have a moderately positive retirement.

■ People who are passive and dependent and who have little interest in the world around them tend to have a moderately negative retirement.

■ Those who were unhappy and dissatisfied through-out life tend also to have a negative retirement.

2. Form an even number of small groups. If you have enough participants to form six groups of 2–4 participants, each group will prepare two role-plays. Give one **Exercise in choice** card to each group. If you give Card 1a to one group, be sure to give card 1b to another because the role-plays should be presented in pairs. Distribute paper and pencils and provide the following instructions:

➤ In your group, ask one person to read aloud the scenario on the **Exercise in choice** card. Some of the cards describe optimistic, positive retirees; other cards describe people with negative attitudes toward retirement.

➤ Select a group recorder to list all your ideas, then

brainstorm comments the person described on your card might make to justify and explain their attitude.

➤ Referring to the recorder's list, develop a 2–3 minute role-play that includes several people from your group. Present your subject's ideas about retirement boldly and with humor. Each role player is to think of someone they know who is very positive or negative in retirement. Consider how they would respond using the clues developed during the brainstorming session. Have fun with this activity and feel free to overact. After 10 minutes, you will have an opportunity to present your play to the entire group.

3. Reconvene the group. Beginning with **Exercise in choice** card 1a, followed by card 1b, and continuing through the rest of the cards, ask participants to present their role-plays. After each pair of role-plays, pause and ask for discussion. Encourage participants to recognize the benefits of a positive attitude, but help them to understand people who have a more negative attitude.

4. Conclude by asking participants for their insights about the difference attitude makes when a major life change is faced.

Variation

■ If the group is small, ask participants to develop only a few role-plays, then continue with a roundtable discussion of the remaining scenarios.

Exercise in choice

1a Choices about independence
Marta wants to be independent and is planning a trip to
Europe. She will visit her old home in Germany, then she
will continue to travel throughout Western Europe on her
own. Her children are concerned about her safety.

1b Choices about independence
Pete feels dependent. For many years, Pete had hinted to
his children that he would like to live with one of them
when he retired. Now that time has come. Pete is ready to
move in, but his children are reluctant.

2a Choices about friends
Karen, the wife of a military officer, moved frequently,
making many acquaintances but few real friends. Now that
she and her husband are settled, she is determined to
develop lots of new friendships.

2b Choices about friends
Elizabeth has a few very good friends whom she has
known for many years. She fears losing them to illness or
death, but she doesn't want to disturb their intimate
relationship by seeking new friends.

3a Choices about money
Although John has enough money to feel secure, he worries
and complains about it all the time. He doesn't want to give
money to his children or to charities, but he also doesn't
want to use it for medical or nursing home care.

3b Choices about money
Matt doesn't have to worry about money, and he doesn't
want to. He made a financial plan while he was still working
and revised it after retirement. Part of his planning included
gifts to his children and to charities that he cares about.

©1997 Whole Person Press 210 W Michigan Duluth MN 55802   (800) 247-6789

Exercise in choice

4a Choices about civic involvement
When Joe retired, he breathed a sigh of relief. As vice president of a small bank, he was expected to take on civic responsibilities. Now he can sit back and let other people attend the meetings and do the work. He's all done.

4b Choices about civic involvement
Mary was a member of many organizations, but her demanding job took lots of time. When she retired, she rolled up her sleeves and got to work, delighted that she finally had time to support groups she cared about.

5a Choices about learning
When Matthew realized that his grandchildren knew more about computers than he did, he signed up for a course at the community college. Now he manages his church's mailing list and creates the monthly newsletter.

5b Choices about learning
Bonnie's husband wants to attend an Elderhostel, but Bonnie thinks she's too old to sit in a classroom and concentrate. She plans to relax during retirement and let the young folks strain their muscles and their brains.

6a Choices about work
Jan has a very tight budget. She was a great cook but the restaurant she worked in didn't offer a pension plan. If she catered a few parties each month, she'd have the extra money she needs, but she would rather scrimp than work.

6b Choices about work
Peter worked as an accountant all his life. Now that he has retired, he works as a volunteer three months each year, preparing taxes for seniors who need his knowledge and assistance.

©1997 Whole Person Press 210 W Michigan Duluth MN 55802 (800) 247-6789

26 Setting goals and reaching them

Setting goals is essential for a successful retirement. In this exercise, individuals work together to set goals and to develop plans for meeting those goals.

Objectives

To begin to organize the process of retirement by setting goals and taking appropriate steps to achieve them.

To be willing to confer with others and use resources as we plan for or try to improve our retirement.

To examine more carefully the base from which we begin planning including family, work, education, spirituality, and others.

To see the need to make, adjust, and remake decisions as a long retirement unfolds.

Group size

Unlimited as long as there is sufficient space for groups of four to work without crowding each other.

Time

40–90 minutes.

Material

Easel pad and markers; paper and pencils.

Process

1. Introduce the exercise with a brief discussion, asking some of the following questions to establish the concept that people set a variety of goals, and they can reach those goals in many ways:

   ✔ What are some of your goals for your retirement years?

✔ Are these goals the same now as they were ten or twenty years ago? If not, how have they changed?

✔ Do your family, friends, and community support your freedom to consider many options? If not, what are some of their concerns?

✔ In what ways has your education, work, and community involvement given you chances to set goals and take risks?

2. Form groups of four participants; distribute paper and pencils; and provide the following instructions, illustrating them as you speak by duplicating on the easel pad the diagram shown below:

Counselor A ○ ○ **Counselor B**
Helps client identify goals
Client ○
Helps client prioritize goals and develop strategies for reaching them

Recorder ○

➤ Today, you will have the opportunity to act as retirement counselors for each other.

➤ Begin by selecting one person from your group to be your retirement counseling firm's client.

➤ Choose another person to act as the group's recorder. This person will take notes on the discussion but should also feel free to participate.

➤ Select one of the two remaining group members to help the client define and state his or her retirement goals. The goals could be in areas such as finance, health, education, service, and spirituality.

➤ After several goals have been listed, the fourth member of your group should help the client identify those

©1997 Whole Person Press 210 W Michigan Duluth MN 55802   (800) 247-6789

that are most important and then should lead the group in brainstorming ways in which the client could reach those goals.

➤ You will have 15 minutes for this process.

3. After 15 minutes, call time. Ask participants to switch roles and begin the process again.

☞ *If you have enough time, the groups can switch roles two more times, giving each person a chance to identify their personal goals and strategies for reaching them.*

4. Reconvene the entire group and select one of the following ways to conclude the session:

■ Ask for short reports from each group.

■ Lead a discussion of goals that participants have set and some of the steps suggested to reach them.

■ Distribute the recorders' notes to each "client" and encourage them to begin implementing the strategies they identified.

27 My life today and five years from now

In this exercise, participants compare their own attitudes and activities to those of other retirees. They consider what kind of life they want five years from now and the steps they should take to achieve this life.

Objectives

To set new long-term goals.

To be less dependent on others and to gain the personal satisfaction that comes from aiding other people and our community.

To free ourselves from the myths of earlier generations and engage in a retirement with a purpose.

Group size

Unlimited.

Time

40 minutes, more if discussion is extended.

Materials

Easel pad and markers; pencils; **My life today and in the future** worksheet; **My activities today and in the future** worksheet.

Process

1. Introduce the theme of planning for an independent retirement by presenting some of the following concepts and information:

   ■ In the past, many people in their sixties stopped productive work, backed out of community involvements, and retired to the bosom of their family. Today, people live longer, and because they have many resources beyond their families, they often make retirement plans independently. This sweeping cultural change requires far more planning for the later years.

■ Service organizations provide positive outlets for volunteers of all ages to be productively involved in their community.

■ Volunteering is as valuable to the volunteers as it is to the individual or group being helped.

■ Self esteem is enhanced by the productive use of leisure time.

■ Our sense of personal value can decline as we disengage from work unless we become involved in worthwhile activities.

■ Continued learning has a positive impact on retirees.

2. Distribute the **My life today and in the future** worksheet and provide the following instructions:

➤ This worksheet will give you a chance to assess your satisfaction with your life today.

➤ For each statement, underline the number that indicates the extent to which you agree with that statement. Underlining the number 1 indicates that you completely disagree with a statement. Underlining the number 7 indicates that you strongly agree with a statement.

➤ After you underline the number that reflects your present satisfaction with life, circle the number that shows how you would like to feel five years from now.

3. After 10 minutes, lead a discussion using some of the following questions:

✔ Were you surprised by what you discovered as you completed the worksheet?

©1997 Whole Person Press 210 W Michigan Duluth MN 55802   (800) 247-6789

✔ In what areas did you find the greatest disparity between where you are now and where you would like to be?

✔ What changes do you need to make to be sure that you will be fully satisfied with your life five years from now?

4. Distribute the **My activities today and in the future** worksheet and provide the following instructions:

➤ Changes in attitude often follow changes in activities. On this worksheet, list your current activities; then think about specific changes you would like to make so that your life will be more satisfying. What should you begin to do differently so that soon you can begin to feel different?

➤ In response to question 5 on the worksheet, list several concrete steps you could begin taking right now to achieve your goals.

5. Conclude the exercise by asking participants to share some of the concrete actions they plan to take.

Variation

■ Several objectives of this exercise can be achieved without group discussion. If time does not permit discussion, participants should be encouraged to examine their own responses, asking themselves what they can do to improve their own retirement plans. Using this simplified version of the exercise, it can be completed in 30 minutes.

My life today and in the future

Underline the number that indicates how you feel right now. Circle the number that shows how you would like to feel five years from now. 1=disagree, 7=complete agreement

1. I'm happy and enjoy life.

1   2   3   4   5   6   7

2. I'm friendly and enjoy being with other people.

1   2   3   4   5   6   7

3. I'm content with my life.

1   2   3   4   5   6   7

4. I'm satisfied with my financial situation.

1   2   3   4   5   6   7

5. I like to work, either as a volunteer or for pay.

1   2   3   4   5   6   7

6. I'm able to live independently and pay my own way.

1   2   3   4   5   6   7

7. I lead a busy, active life.

1   2   3   4   5   6   7

8. I'm committed to at least one important cause.

1   2   3   4   5   6   7

9. I enjoy learning and keep mentally active.

1   2   3   4   5   6   7

10. It's important for me to maintain my individuality.

1   2   3   4   5   6   7

11. I have a deeply satisfying spiritual life.

1   2   3   4   5   6   7

12. I'm involved in improving my community.

1   2   3   4   5   6   7

©1997 Whole Person Press 210 W Michigan Duluth MN 55802   (800) 247-6789

My activities today and in the future

1. What hobbies were you involved in this past year?

   _____

   What hobbies do you expect to have five years from now?

   _____

2. How many hours per week do you take part in physical activities (walking, swimming, golfing, etc.)? _____

   Five years from now, how many hours per week do you think you should participate in activities?_____

3. What work did you do for pay during the past year?

   _____

   Work not for pay? _____

   What work would you like to be doing for pay five years from now? _____

   Work not for pay? _____

4. What formal and informal programs of learning were you involved in during the past year? _____

   _____

   What programs of learning would you like to be involved in five years from now? _____

   _____

5. List several concrete steps you could begin taking right now to insure a more satisfying retirement.

   _____

   _____

   _____

©1997 Whole Person Press 210 W Michigan Duluth MN 55802   (800) 247-6789

28 Energy for life

In this exercise, participants determine how much energy they have left after completing their tasks, and they explore ways of increasing their energy.

Objectives

To be realistic in determining the energy necessary for a new task.

To consider the type of energy—physical, intellectual, social, or spiritual—required by various tasks.

To find ways to increase our energy before accepting new responsibilities.

To be considerate of other people's energy before loading them down with extra work.

Group size

30 is ideal, has been used with over 100 participants.

Time

30–40 minutes, 60 minutes with large groups.

Materials

Easel pad and markers; pencils; **Energy audit** worksheet.

Process

1. Introduce the exercise by telling the story of Charles.

   Charles, a usually strong and vigorous man, returned home after hospitalization for cancer. He had not fully recovered from the disease or from the treatments. After a few days of rest, he decided to mow the lawn. Much to his dismay, he was exhausted after just 30 minutes of pushing the lawn mower. Discouraged, he told his wife, "I just can't do this today. I'm done in after only half an hour."

©1997 Whole Person Press 210 W Michigan Duluth MN 55802 (800) 247-6789

2. Lead a discussion of the energy needed for a good life, making the comments below. The analogy of a rechargeable battery might help clarify the concept of draining and recharging. As you talk about the units of energy, work the subtraction on the easel pad.

- We each have many kinds of energy: physical, intellectual, emotional, spiritual, social, and vocational. Our energy level in each area varies throughout life.

- At the height of youthful good health, Charles could be described as having 100 units of physical energy.

- Although he has continued to exercise, his energy diminished somewhat with age. Now, when he is healthy and rested, he has about 80 units of physical energy.

- Charles's illness and treatments have put a tremendous load on him, draining 65 units of energy. Before he began mowing the lawn, he had a balance of only 15 units of physical energy available. That was used up quickly, leaving him exhausted.

- There are two ways to increase your energy balance: either recharge yourself with fresh energy, or cut down on the load that is draining your energy.

3. Ask participants to provide an example of the drain on intellectual, emotional, spiritual, social, or vocational energy as you work out the subtraction on the easel pad.

4. Distribute the **Energy audit** worksheet and provide the following instructions, giving time between the steps for participants to complete them.

➤ In the first column of the worksheet, several kinds of energy are listed. Add any others that are important to you.

➤ In the second column, record your current level of physical, intellectual, vocational, emotional, spiritual, and social energy. That's the level you have when you're feeling healthy, relaxed, and optimistic. If you believe that during those times your intellectual energy is as good as it ever was, rate it 100. When you consider your social energy, if you know it is well below what it was twenty years ago, rate it 60 or 70.

➤ In the next column, record any recent load on your energy. The death of a spouse, for instance, might drain you of 70 or 80 units of emotional energy. Moving into a new home could drain you of physical, emotional, and social energy.

➤ Subtract your recent energy load from your current energy level to determine how much energy you have available in each area. If your current level of social energy is 60 and, due to the closing of your senior club, you were drained of 60 units of energy, no balance remains. This could be a problem for you.

➤ Finally, complete the questions at the bottom of the worksheet.

5. After 10 minutes, lead a discussion of the worksheet, using some of the questions below. Be sure that the discussion touches on each of the energy areas.

   ✔ For what activities do you want to have plenty of energy?

   ✔ As we age, is it more likely that we will increase our energy or decrease the drain on it? Which would you try to do?

   ✔ What can we do to increase our level of energy?

   ✔ What are examples of ways we can reduce any load that drains too much energy?

6. Conclude the discussion by encouraging participants to live energetically and enthusiastically and to keep a bit of balance in their lives.

Variation

■ During the discussion, ask participants to share examples from their own lives of times when they have deliberately attempted to increase their energy by physical conditioning, learning new skills, obtaining help from a psychologist, or conferring with a spiritual leader.

The exercise is based on a concept developed by Howard McClusky at the University of Michigan.

Energy audit

Use this worksheet to help you think about the energy you have for life. Assume that at one time your maximum energy was 100 units in each of the areas listed below. It may still be at that level.

In column two, estimate and enter the units of energy you now have in relation to a maximum of 100. In column three, estimate and enter the recent heaviest load required for each kind of energy. In column four, use the formula (energy – load = balance) to determine your balance, and enter it in your chart.

Kind of energy	Current level of energy	Recent load or drain	Your balance
Physical			
Intellectual			
Vocational			
Emotional			
Spiritual			
Social			
Other (write in)			

In which of the above areas have you often approached zero balance?

In which area do you have the highest balance?

©1997 Whole Person Press 210 W Michigan Duluth MN 55802   (800) 247-6789

29 Advice from positive retirees

Those who retire well look forward, not back. They accept life without growling about it, and they live for tomorrow. As participants consider the advice offered by several positive retirees, they will also consider how they can enrich their own retirement.

Objectives

To look for more positive ways to respond to the special pressures that come with aging.

To consider how we can avoid decline and encourage personal growth in ourselves and others.

Group size

10–30 participants.

Time

50 minutes.

Materials

The **Nine characteristics of those having a positive retirement** handout; **Advice cards**.

Process

1. Distribute the **Nine characteristics of people having a positive retirement** handout and introduce the exercise with the following comments:

   ■ Prior to their own retirement, Burt and Doris Kreitlow interviewed 140 persons selected by others as very positive retirees.

   ■ The 140 positive retirees had many of the following characteristics in common: They were sociable, volunteered their time and resources, kept active, were happy, looked ahead, tried to be independent, continued to learn, had a strong work ethic, and stayed involved in their community.

■ Other research has shown that those who retire well accept life without grumbling and live for tomorrow. They seek activities outside of themselves.

■ People who retire well have a purpose in their lives, a purpose that goes beyond thinking only of themselves.

■ Purposeful living gets people past the day-to-day problems of retirement.

■ The 140 positive retirees looked to the future and found that retirement was the best time of their lives.

2. Form nine small groups and distribute a photocopy of one **Advice card** to each group.

☞ *If you have fewer than eighteen participants, give each group two or more cards.*

3. Ask participants to study and discuss the advice and prepare to report their insights to the entire group. The following questions will help participants focus their report.

✔ Have you ever had a need for this kind of advice?

✔ Do you know anyone else who may need it?

✔ Would you feel comfortable giving this kind of advice to friends or family?

✔ Why are some retired folks hesitant to listen to suggestions about how to improve their own retirement?

4. Reconvene the entire group and conclude the exercise with a brief discussion of each retiree's advice.

Variation

■ A series of club or senior center programs could be developed from the advice of positive retirees.

The nine characteristics
of those having a positive retirement

1. They volunteer—providing service to others; generously sharing their energy, resources, and time; demonstrating concern for other persons, groups, and the larger community.

2. They like people—are sociable, kind, loving, and willing to get along with everyone.

3. They are busy and active—searching for things to do, participating in hobbies, and having broad interests.

4. They are happy and content—calm even with turmoil around them, enjoying life fully, outgoing and even-tempered.

5. They are forward looking—positive in their outlook, optimistic, creative, and open-minded.

6. They are independent—trying to pay their own way, do their own thing, and take things "free and easy," but are assertive when necessary.

7. They are continuing learners—loving to learn, curious about the unknown, choosing to keep their minds active.

8. They are workers—demonstrating the work ethic, laboring tirelessly when there is a task to do, willing to begin new projects.

9. They are civic-minded—involved in community affairs, willing to lead or to follow, eager to commit themselves to community goals.

©1997 Whole Person Press 210 W Michigan Duluth MN 55802 · (800) 247-6789

Advice cards

1. Volunteer.

Andy Harper, a retired North Carolina businessman, responded as follows, "I tell them to get involved in things that will make their life more worthwhile. Volunteering will bring a lot of happiness. I like to help other retired persons take their first step. After that, they can walk alone."

2. Get involved with others.

Rose Clayton, a member of an English Pensioner's Club, responded, "I tell people to go out a lot. Check into the 'Over Sixties' and other clubs in your area. Go dancing; it keeps the limbs moving. Do something. Don't sit and mope. If you keep sitting about, the bones don't want to get moving again. My next door neighbor was that way, and I got her out. She didn't know what social life was like until I moved in next door to her. I don't believe in going and taking things to her or sitting and talking and having tea. I asked her to go with me to the club for a dance. She asked if her sister could go too, and soon there were eight of us going. That's how I got her out of the house."

©1997 Whole Person Press 210 W Michigan Duluth MN 55802   (800) 247-6789

Advice cards

3. Be busy and active.

Mrs. Kanahele in Hawaii is a sprightly 63-year-old of Hawaiian-Chinese ancestry who raised six children and worked off and on since age six. Her son insisted that she retire, but she hasn't slowed down. In response to the question, she said. "I say to them, 'Come, let's go,' and ask them to go out with me. When my husband retired, he wanted to stay home and play with his artifacts. I would look at him and say, 'Gee, you sit here all day long, come out and meet people other than those from church.' He is a retired minister. Staying home isn't enough. People should look for something to do outside of the home. You get stale if you are cooped up in the house."

4. Seek happiness and contentment.

Lisa Bell, age 74, came north at age 62 with her eight children. She is a product of the southern black culture and worked regularly until retirement. Her answer, "I would give advice sometimes. If they are harsh, I speak to them and tell them, 'You gotta smile.' Whether you feel like smiling or not, you still gotta smile. Kind words gain people. You don't gain no peoples by talking harsh. It's good for them."

Advice cards

5. Look ahead.

Bernie Andrews retired from a Wisconsin farm but continued his civic involvement and took on part-time jobs such as town clerk and census director. His advice is for retirees to look ahead, not back. He says, "I tell them to stop living in the past. Enjoy today and plan for tomorrow. Go back to school if necessary to get your mind off the past. If they take classes, they quit being selfish. Even accomplished people sometimes forget how important it is to look ahead."

6. Be independent.

Wanda Edwards retired from a job in survey research and moved to North Carolina. She and new friends took computer science classes at a university, took part-time jobs, and then learned to swim and golf. Wanda's independent lifestyle is demonstrated in the advice she gives to others. "I tell them to get out and do things for themselves. Take advantage of every opportunity. Forget your age and move it! If you're bored, try something else. Do what I did. I didn't retire *from* something, I retired *to* something. Get going!"

Advice cards

7. Continue to learn.

Harry Everett, dockworker, school caretaker, and worker in the school's welfare office, joined his wife in entertaining at senior clubs and meetings in a large English city. When asked for advice he said, "To people who ask, 'What's your secret?' I say there is no secret. Keep your body and mind active and for goodness sake, don't go sit before the fire. Get up and get out and about. Some say that they don't know how to dance so I say, 'Come out and learn.' I honestly believe that is the secret of keeping going, and many have followed it. Oh yes, the worst thing for a person of 65 is to say, 'That's it, that's the finish.' Its daft to say that. That's the worst."

8. Be a worker.

Sam Rist retired after forty years with a county highway department in Minnesota. He volunteers at his senior center and encourages others to work there too. His example: "There's a widow who has been in the nursing home for a year, but when we got the senior center going, we encouraged her to join us. She came out and never went back to the home. The center is the key for some people. This lady changed, she's better now. She had gone slack. When she saw that the center needed help, she came down to help and is again the worker she used to be."

Advice cards

9.Be active in your community.

Sidney Talbott retired from both the Royal Navy and later from a management position in nuclear engineering. Always a participant in civic affairs, he had chaired important committees and been a mayor. He believes that involvement in civic and community activities is an inherent quality, and it won't help to give advice. He says, "No advice. It's not inherent in them. They are happy being cabbages. Why upset or disturb them? There's too much telling people what they should do. Make them aware of the situation, then stop."

How to use this book
most effectively

The concept of experiential learning

As you will notice with just a cursory glance through this volume, these educational experiences actively involve participants in the learning process. Why? Because when you draw on the resources of the group in your presentations, you empower people.

Every session in this book balances information and group participation. These exercises concentrate on developing awareness and understanding plus building skills that can be used in all areas of life. This model helps participants become involved and therefore makes it more likely they will assume responsibility for their own learning.

Each exercise is designed to create opportunities for participants to interact with the concepts and each other in meaningful ways. The lecture method is usually replaced with facilitative questions that guide group members to discover their own answers. The authority of the leader is transformed into the wisdom of the group.

The leader's challenge

For many teachers, giving up the authority implicit in the typical lecture format is a risky proposition. Teachers are often afraid that they won't be perceived as an expert, so they are tempted to lecture, entertain, and keep the focus on themselves. Yet, if your goal as a leader is truly to help people change, information is not enough. Praise from your audience is not enough. What really counts are the discoveries that you and the group members make together about your current lifestyles and the choices you can make now to prepare for a great retirement.

Remember, as a leader, you are not presenting a paper at a conference. You are engaging your group in an educational process. Your task is to appeal to people with different learning styles, using a wide variety of strategies so all are involved. In whole person learning, the questions are as important as the content.

The strategies for leading a group

These exercises help you involve people in the process of reflecting, prioritizing, sorting, and planning for change by using the strategies listed below. As you prepare and lead groups, remember that you are a participant and a learner as well as a leader.

1. **Activating participants' internal wisdom:** This is best accomplished by asking questions that help people come up with answers that are right for them, rather than by giving them your "right answers."

2. **Helping people make choices:** These exercises assist people to sort out their own values and priorities, helping them to explore their beliefs and assumptions and encouraging them to alter their lives in ways that they choose, based on their own sense of rhythm and timing.

3. **Activating the group's resources:** These exercises take the dynamic of the group seriously. The first five minutes are the key! They help you get people involved with each other right off the bat and let you use and work with the energy of the group—the laughter, the group norms, the embarrassment, the competition.

4. **Fostering interpersonal support:** With these exercises you capitalize on the rich variety of experiences and insights among your participants. And you capitalize on the power of their support for each other. Interaction builds trust, helps people consider new options, and offers support for change. For many people, this chance to compare notes with others is the most powerful part of the session.

The rhythm of each session

Each exercise is designed to include a rhythmic sequence of activities with enough change of pace to keep the group's involvement and energy high. Most exercises include:

A chalktalk—A brief introduction to the session's main concepts.

Personal reflection—Questions to help each participant test the concepts against their own life experiences in order to determine which ideas make sense to them.

A summary—A pooling of the group's observations and insights.

Planning/commitment—The bottom line in training. Everyone should leave the session with at least one clear idea about what they will do next.

The format

The format of this book is designed for easy use. Every exercise is described completely, including goals, group size, time, materials needed, step-by-step process instructions, and variations. The format employs the following symbols to help indicate specific items:

☞*Special instructions for the leader are set in italics and preceded by a pointing hand.*

✔ Questions to ask participants are preceded by a check.

➤ Instructions for group activities are indicated by an arrow.

■ Chalktalk (mini-lecture) notes are preceded by a bullet.

Time: The time frame provided at the beginning of each exercise and times given for various activities within the process are only guidelines—suggestions to help you organize and schedule a successful workshop. Because time

©1997 Whole Person Press 210 W Michigan Duluth MN 55802   (800) 247-6789

pressures can make older adults feel tense and uncomfortable, avoid announcing time limits for individual work.

Worksheets: Many of the exercises include worksheets for participants to complete. The worksheets can be found immediately following the exercises in which they are to be used. Make certain you photocopy enough worksheets prior to conducting an exercise. (8 ½" x 11" photocopy masters for this book are also available from Whole Person Associates.)

Chalktalks: Many of the exercises include chalktalk notes—bulleted lists of information that help introduce an exercise or provide vital information on its topic. These notes provide a framework to help you develop a complete mini-lecture of your own.

Tips for using these exercises most effectively

1. **Tailor your process to the group:** Read the objectives for each exercise and carefully choose those you will use. Decide what is appropriate based on the setting, the time available, the purpose, and the participants' style and comfort level. Exercises should be specifically selected for a particular group and should be tailored to that group's style and culture. What will work well in one situation may not work as effectively in another. Feel free to adapt exercises as you deem necessary.

2. **Pay attention to the timing:** In your planning, anticipate the needs and rhythm of the group. At the first session, you'll need more time for getting acquainted. In later sessions, as you all get to know each other better you'll need to allocate more time for the discussion segments.

   Every group goes through predictable (and unpredictable!) cycles. Anticipate peak times and down times and plan for changing the pace as needed to restore energy and enthusiasm.

3. Prepare yourself thoroughly for each session: Good teaching is built on examples and anecdotes. In order to make the material come alive for you and for others, you will need to carefully work through each session and personalize each segment with your own examples and stories. You can do this in a number of ways:

- Read the detailed exercise outline thoroughly. Be sure you understand the basic concepts and processes for the session. Answer all worksheet questions for yourself. This will help you anticipate difficulties and will provide you with lively personal examples.

- Reread the chalktalk notes one point at a time. Translate the ideas into your own words. Personalize each concept with carefully chosen examples that you think will fit the group's needs.

- Add diagrams, cartoons, newspaper articles—whatever relevant information you come across during your preparation.

- Relax. Take a few minutes by yourself before you begin each session so that you are centered and focused.

4. Make the environment work for you: The room makes a very important contribution to the atmosphere. The best location has soft lighting, comfortable chairs, is neither too big nor too small, and has privacy to prevent interruptions that would distract the group. If you must meet in a room that's too large, keep the group together.

Banked auditoriums with fixed seats are workable, but not recommended. The inflexibility of the seating makes small group gatherings more difficult.

Encourage participants to sit in a circle. This creates the most successful setting since it provides an ideal

©1997 Whole Person Press 210 W Michigan Duluth MN 55802   (800) 247-6789

forum for verbal and nonverbal communication and offers an atmosphere of inclusion.

You will want to have an easel pad or chalkboard available for your use at all times.

Don't expect anyone else to set up the room for you. Get there early and, if necessary, set it up yourself.

5. **Establish a supportive atmosphere:** Everyone in the group must feel safe enough to examine their attitudes and beliefs and to change some of them. A leader open to listening to everyone's ideas creates an atmosphere of security.

Always restate a participant's comment or question before you respond. Summarizing what you heard affirms the person and shows your audience that you are listening and taking them seriously.

Begin the workshop with a discussion of guidelines for the session. This helps alleviate anxiety and sets a positive tone. Suggestions include: listen to each other carefully and respect confidentiality.

6. **Carefully plan the small group discussions:** For most discussions, groups of four to six are optimal. Timing will be a problem if some groups have three people and others have eight. So try to keep groups the same size as indicated in the instructions.

If some people don't participate (or even leave the room during group sharing time) don't panic. Don't drop the group experience because a few people feel uncomfortable. For many people the small group discussions are the most valuable part of the session.

7. **Grow from this experience yourself:** Try to learn the most you can from every event. Don't be afraid to share

yourself. Remember that you are both a leader and a participant!

Don't be discouraged if each session does not go exactly as you had expected. Turn disasters into opportunities. When something does not go well, laugh! When all else fails, start asking questions.

Plan to have fun! The processes in these exercises are designed so that you have a chance to listen as well as talk. The whole experience does not depend on you. Open your eyes and your ears, you'll learn something too!